Talk Your Head Off

(…and Write, Too!)

written by **Brana Rish West**

illustrated by **Harlan West**

Longman

Library of Congress Cataloguing-in-Publication Data

West, Brana Rish
     Talk your head off (--and write, too!) / written by Brana Rish
West ; illustrated by Harlan West.
         p.   cm.
     Includes index.
     ISBN 0-13-476201-0
     1. English language--Textbooks for foreign speakers.   2. English
language--spoken English.   3. English language--Rhetoric.   I. West,
Harlan.   II. Title
PE1128.W429   1996
428.2'4--dc20
                                                    96-27295
                                                        CIP

Publisher: *Louisa B. Hellegers*
Development Editor: *Barbara Barysh*
Production Editor: *Ken Liao*
Art Director: *Merle Krumper*

Compositor: *Harlan West Design*
Cover art: *Harlan West*

Printed in the United States of America

10   9

ISBN 0-13-476201-0

Table of Contents

Table of Contents

Table of Contents

Table of Contents

Table of Contents

Foreword

Talk Your Head Off is the kind of book students and teachers have been talking about for a long time. Students want to learn to speak English. Teachers want a book that simplifies the learning process while making it a unique and enjoyable experience. *Talk Your Head Off* accomplishes both of these goals and more!

After studying the beginning levels in English, students have acquired enough basic vocabulary and pronunciation skills to produce sentences with their own ideas and opinions. They have the ability to have conversations; they just need the confidence and practice. Practice they find interesting and fun.

My students constantly ask me, "Teacher, how can I learn to speak English?" I answer them with a few questions such as, "How did you learn to drive?" or "How did you learn to walk?" or, for that matter, "How did you learn to speak your first language?" The answer to all the questions, both theirs and mine, was "You just do it!" We learn to speak by speaking: not by repeating drills, but by forming original sentences through original ideas. Interesting and meaningful conversational topics, with lead questions, make this possible.

The students will neither have perfect grammar nor precise pronunciation at the onset of instruction, but that is why they have a teacher who is there to correct, interpret, instruct, and facilitate their learning process. As an intermediate or advanced ESL teacher you step back and guide students through their original thought processes. With this method of instruction students not only learn to speak quickly, but they are also very enthusiastic about the conversational topics. They can't wait to find out what they are going to talk about, so attendance soars. Not only that, you will find yourself enjoying the class as much as your students do, as you learn different facts, trivia, and students' opinions on a variety of subjects.

Research shows that small-group and pair work dramatically increase the learning process. Nevertheless, one cannot just write questions on the board and hope the students will talk. Putting any group of strangers into a circle and asking them to converse in any language is a difficult task. Some people might not talk because they feel they would be judged, others might be shy, but most would be embarrassed to talk to people they have never met before. Now, if you add lack of language proficiency to the above, you have quite a task getting your group of complete strangers with limited language proficiency to speak. The key here is complete strangers. Once people know each other, or at least feel like they know each other, they will be willing to converse on a variety of topics in groups. And, once people feel comfortable in their groups, they can and do help each other fill in the gaps in their language abilities.

To get to know someone one must begin with non-threatening questions, usually based solely on facts, and then build to more subjective questions formed through opinions. Examples of fact questions may be, "What is your name?" or "What is the person next to you wearing?" After learning some facts about each other, the students will be ready to answer more socially sensitive and thought provoking questions such as, "Why do some people get divorced?" or "What are some ways people define success?" Finally, and perhaps the most difficult of all, come the opinion questions such as, "Do you think a government has the right to enforce capital punishment?" Why or why not?"

Foreword

This book helps students learn how to express their opinions and ideas. It does so by forging the path from simplified to more complicated questions to teach students how to feel comfortable speaking in English. The book's order is pertinent, so it's best not to skip around.

There are five sections to each lesson in the book: *Vocabulary, Usage, Let's Start, Let's Talk,* and an *Exercise and Activities* page.

The vocabulary section is divided into *New Words* and *Let's Talk Words*. The *New Words* are the words on the first page of the lesson. They are used to help get the students acquainted with the topic. The *Let's Talk Words* are topic related as well and give students the vocabulary necessary to produce their own original sentences for the *Let's Talk* section. All the vocabulary is pertinent, and all words should be pronounced, defined, and briefly explained to the students. This can be done by using example sentences, pictures, pantomime, or role play. In some lessons space has been provided so students can add their own relevant vocabulary.

The *Usage* section helps students become acquainted with the vocabulary words through matching exercises, defining and drawing exercises, writing exercises, and games. This section gives students practice using the vocabulary words. The exercises are meant for group, pair, or class practice. The students help each other use and understand the meaning of the words through activities. The activities are eclectic to prevent boredom, and, at the same time, accommodate various learners' styles.

Let's Start provides activities that encourage students to get ready for conversing. Talking in groups or as a class, sharing ideas, using one's imagination, and speaking are the elements that comprise this section.

The *Let's Talk* section is the core of the text. To work in the *Let's Talk* section students should be in groups of four to six. This section is filled with adult topics, and questions geared specifically for adults. The topics increase in difficulty not only grammatically, but in social sensitivity as well. The questions in this section lead the students into forming original sentences that stem from their own opinions and beliefs. There are no correct answers to the majority of the questions: The questions are meant to promote conversation. The teacher listens to what students say and determines when grammatical corrections are necessary. If the student is understood, but forgets an article, the student is generally not corrected; however, if the student is not understood by a native speaker, or could be misunderstood, then a correction is necessary. You must remember that it isn't the correction that embarrasses the student, but how that correction is delivered. You could say, "Your opinion is very interesting. The way most English speakers say that is . . . (or) People would understand you better if you said . . . ." Students not only appreciate such corrections, but they expect the teacher to correct them when their grammar or pronunciation prevents communication.

Finally, to close each lesson, there is an *Exercises and Activities* page where students take surveys, write their thoughts, and expand on the topics. The survey section encourages students to meet and converse with other students, gives additional practice in creative speaking and listening, and allows the students writing practice.

Now that I've "talked your head off," please go to the first topic and begin. And when your students ask you how they can improve their English—just tell them to "Talk Your Head Off!"

To the Teacher

Developing a textbook that elicits authentic language instead of *textbook talk* (drills or exercises that have preordained answers) presents many difficulties. Should the book be written as one speaks? If so, what kind of speech (formal or informal)? Common everyday spoken English is filled with grammatical inconsistencies that traditional prescriptive grammarians would identify as errors. Linguists, on the other hand, view language as ever changing and therefore write their grammatical rules to fit the spoken language that is used.

This book implements a liberal and conversational grammatical structure. Prepositions occur at the end of sentences since they are rarely, if ever, at the beginning in spoken English. Contractions are used, since they are conversational, and they usually do not violate standard English rules.

When looking at the grammar focus in the lessons, the structure might not be as apparent as in some grammar books. The structural foci are carefully embedded into the lessons to have students answer using the correct forms. Teachers act as facilitators to help students produce the forms. Many of the lessons demonstrate new grammatical experiences for the students; however, in all lessons, previous grammatical structures are used. Therefore, each lesson contains a multiplicity of grammatical forms. Furthermore, from lesson to lesson, the book gradually increases in grammatical complexity. The idea is *not* to have students practice one grammatical form at a time, but rather to continue what they know while introducing new structures. "Real world English" involves a conglomeration of grammatical structures even within basic conversations. Students need to practice speaking the way native English speakers speak rather than practicing one structure at a time. Thus, this book gives conversation practice that is as close as possible to "real world speech."

Acknowledgments

We would like to thank the people who helped develop and produce this textbook. We appreciate the teamwork dedicated by Prentice Hall Regents to help us through the publishing process. Thank you, Arley Gray, for granting us the opportunity to work with your team of experts. We appreciate all the feedback and guidance we received from Louisa Hellegers, Ken Liao, and Sheryl Olinsky. We are especially grateful for the help of Barbara Barysh, our editor, who oversaw the complete process of the book from development through production. Without her dedication, expertise, and experience—coupled with kindness, encouragement, and guidance—this book would never have been published.

In addition we want to thank our family, friends, and colleagues for their unlimited enthusiasm, encouragement, and help in getting this book published. Thank you Paul Hamel, Mike Bennett, Jean Owensby, Marvin and Dorothy Rish, Alan West and Lois Fine, David Rish, Nathan Rish, Ethel Rish, Adam West, Stacie Steinberg, Wendy Rosenthal LeBlang, and Chagall and Cotton West.

Brana and Harlan West

This book is dedicated to the memory of Joyce West, a loving mother and teacher who inspired us to achieve.

Lesson 1   Introductions

Vocabulary New Words

country	meet
do	month
have	name
how long	say
introduce	see
am	is	speak
are	language	what
been	learn	where

Let's Talk Words

city	mark (check)
class	married
community	same as
different from	share
else	single
job	study
like	travel
live	visit

Usage

Read the dialog and circle the new words. Then practice the dialog with a partner using your own information.

Jose: Hi. What's your name?

Keiko: (My name's) Keiko.

Jose: I'm Jose. I haven't seen you in this school before.

Keiko: This is my first year here.

Jose: Where are you from?

Keiko: (I'm from) Tokyo, Japan.

Jose: How long have you been in this country?

Keiko: (I've been here for) ten months.

Jose: What languages do you speak?

Keiko: (I speak) Japanese and a little English.

Jose: It's nice to meet you.

Keiko: Nice to meet you too.

Let's Start

Learn each other's names by playing the Name Tag Game. The first student introduces himself to the class by saying, "My name is ___Carlos___, and I'm from ___Mexico___." The next student says, "The first student's name is ___Carlos___, and he's from ___Mexico___. My name is ___Mariko___, and I'm from ___Japan___." The third student will continue by saying, "The first student's name is ___Carlos___ and he's from ___Mexico___. The second student's name is ___Mariko___ and she's from ___Japan___, and my name is _____, and I'm from _____." (Continue until all students have spoken.)

Let's Talk...

1. What's your name?

2. Where are you from?

3. Where do you live now? How long have you lived there?

4. What languages do you speak?

5. How long have you studied English? Where have you studied it?

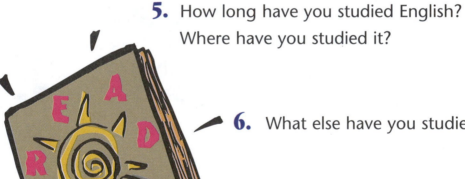

6. What else have you studied?

7. How long have you been at this school?

8. What do you like to do after class?

9. What else do you do?

10. Are you single or married?

11. Talk about where you live now. Describe your community and your city.

12. What countries have you visited? Share your experiences.

13. What do you know about the United States? What do you like about it? What don't you like about it?

A. Survey

Interview students. Meet new people. Complete the chart.

Name	Native country	How long did you live there?	Where do you live now?	Where have you traveled?

Who lives near you now? Who has traveled to the same places that you have visited?

B. Write

Write the names of as many different countries as you can. If necessary, ask your teacher to help spell the names. Circle the countries that you have lived in or visited. Mark the box with the **X** next to the countries where someone in your class has lived. Mark the box with the ✔ next to the countries where someone in your class has traveled.

	X ✔		X ✔		X ✔
_____	☐ ☐	_____	☐ ☐	_____	☐ ☐
_____	☐ ☐	_____	☐ ☐	_____	☐ ☐
_____	☐ ☐	_____	☐ ☐	_____	☐ ☐
_____	☐ ☐	_____	☐ ☐	_____	☐ ☐
_____	☐ ☐	_____	☐ ☐	_____	☐ ☐

C. Fill in

Identification Card

Name _____

Address _____

Native country _____   How long at present address _____

Home telephone_____   Work telephone _____

Emergency telephone _____   Relationship _____

Lesson 2   Favorite Things

Vocabulary New Words

breakfast	lunch
child	meal
dinner	play
eat	sport
favorite	sporting event
go	thing
kind of	

Let's Talk Words

actor	put
actress	singer
ethnic	which
hobby	_____
player	_____
popular	_____
	_____

Usage   Guess your vocabulary words from the clues.

1. meal after lunch: _____
2. like the most: _____
3. baby, young person: _____
4. take part in a sport: _____
5. leave; travel by bus, car, plane: _____
6. Super Bowl, World Series: _____
7. type of: _____
8. put food in your mouth: _____
9. meal before lunch: _____
10. baseball, soccer, football: _____

Write sentences using some of the *Let's Talk* words.

1. _____
2. _____
3. _____
4. _____

Let's Start

Listen. Raise your hand when you hear your favorite thing. Look around the room. How many students have raised their hands? Write the number. Which students have raised their hands? Introduce yourself to these students after class.

Sport:	baseball _____	soccer _____	football _____
Drink:	coffee _____	tea _____	water _____
Meal:	breakfast _____	lunch_____	dinner _____
Entertainment:	TV _____	dancing _____	movies _____

Let's Talk...

1. What kinds of sporting events do you like? Who are your favorite players? Why?

2. What are your favorite TV programs?

3. What is the most popular TV program in your country? Who's your favorite TV actor? Who's your favorite TV actress?

4. What radio station do you listen to? Why?

5. What's your favorite kind of music? Who's your favorite singer? Do you think that person is going to be popular in ten years? Why or why not?

6. What types of sports did you play or watch when you were a child?

7. What types of books did you like to read when you were younger? What were they about?

8. What are some of your favorite hobbies? Name at least five. Which ones are you planning to continue doing in the future? Why?

9. What movies have you seen recently? Talk about one of them. Who's your favorite movie actor? Actress? Why?

10. What kinds of ethnic foods have you eaten? Which have you liked? Which haven't you liked?

11. Have you gone to any restaurants this month? Which ones? What's your favorite food?

A. Survey

What are some of your favorite things? Talk to students in your class and ask them about their favorite colors, sports, music, foods, numbers, seasons, and animals. Write the student's name in the space if the answer is on the chart. If not, add new items to complete the chart.

Things	Favorite	Name	Favorite	Name
colors	*pink*			
sports	*baseball*			
music	*rock*			
foods	*Chinese*			
numbers	*7*			
seasons	*summer*			
animals	*dog*			

What are the most popular items? Discuss with the class.

B. Fill In

What about you? Fill in *your* favorites. Finish the list.

1. color _____

2. sport _____

3. music _____

4. food _____

5. number _____

6. season _____

7. animal _____

8. book _____

9. _____

10. _____

C. Discuss

Work with a partner. Compare your favorite things in Exercise **B**. What do you have in common with your partner?

Lesson 3   Diet and Exercise

Vocabulary New Words

balanced diet	kick
dairy	leg
draw	meat
drink	snack
elbow	stand up
exercise (routine)	toe
fast food	touch
food	twist
fruit	vegetable
jump	vitamin
junk food	waist

Let's Talk Words

ankle	hand	perfect
arm	head	balance
back	if not	shoulder
become	if so	stay
bread	knee	stomach
certain	lose	take
diet	low fat	think
discuss	make	vegetarian
eye	neck	was
food group	nutritious food	weight
foot	overweight	were

Usage

Work with a group.

A. Draw a person and label the body parts.

In your notebooks draw a person and label the body parts listed above. Add any more parts that you know.

B. Are all of these foods part of a balanced diet?

Write an example for each.

1. fruit _____
2. vegetable _____
3. meat _____
4. junk food _____
5. bread _____

6. snack _____
7. fast food _____
8. dairy _____
9. vitamin _____
10. drink _____

Compare your choices with someone in class.

Let's Start

Read the exercise routine below. Then write your own exercise routine with a group. Read it to the class, and have the students do the routine.

Stand up. Touch your toes. Stand up. Jump. Kick with your right leg. Now your left leg. Twist your waist.

Our Exercise routine:

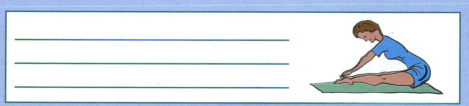

Let's Talk...

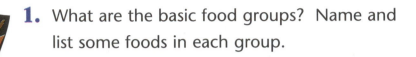

1. What are the basic food groups? Name and list some foods in each group.

2. What is a balanced diet? Give an example.

3. What nutritious foods do you eat? Talk about a healthy meal that you have eaten recently.

4. Do you eat any low-fat foods? If so, what are they? If not, why not?

5. What junk foods and snacks do you like to eat? When do you eat them?

6. What fast foods do you eat? Do you think fast foods are junk foods? Why or why not?

7. What is a vegetarian? Name three reasons people are or become vegetarians. Do you think it is healthy to be a vegetarian? Why or why not?

8. What did your parents tell you to do to stay healthy? Did they tell you to "Eat your vegetables!"?

9. Your overweight friend is on a diet. Tell your friend ten foods not to eat. For example, "Don't eat fried foods!"

10. Name ten types of exercises. Which of these exercises do you do?

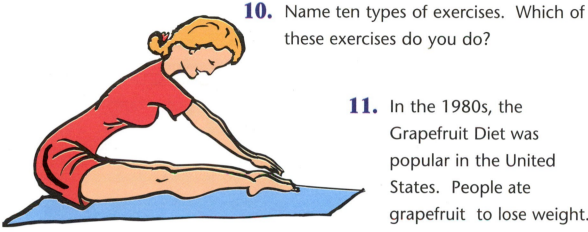

11. In the 1980s, the Grapefruit Diet was popular in the United States. People ate grapefruit to lose weight. What diet foods are popular in your country?

12. Have you ever taken vitamins? Do you think that they are important for a healthy diet? Why or why not?

13. How has your diet changed over the past ten years? What new foods have you eaten recently? What foods don't you eat anymore? Why?

14. How can people lose weight and stay healthy? Discuss your ideas about the perfect balancing of diet and exercise.

A. Survey

Talk to students in your class about diet and exercise.

Name	Favorite exercise	Favorite nutritious food	Favorite fruit	Favorite vegetable

What's the most popular exercise? Nutritious food? Fruit? Vegetable?

B. Write

Ask other students about their eating habits. Write the names of students who fit the descriptions.

_____ is a vegetarian. _____ eats a lot of junk food. _____ doesn't like fish.

_____ takes vitamins. _____ has eaten fast food for lunch. _____ is on a diet.

C. List

What do you eat during the week? Write your shopping list. Share it with a partner. Work together and circle all the healthy foods. Look at the foods you didn't circle. Explain to your partner why you buy certain foods.

_____ _____ _____ _____

_____ _____ _____ _____

D. Fill in

Do you have a friend who wants to lose weight? Do you know someone who's on a special diet? Make a seven-day meal plan for that person. Share your ideas with a few students in your class.

	Sunday	Monday	Tuesday	Wednesday	Thursday	Friday	Saturday
Breakfast							
Lunch							
Dinner							

Lesson 4   Transportation Systems

Vocabulary

bus
can
carpool
drive
fly

New Words

might
passenger
plane
ride
situation
train
transportation system
use
will

***Let's Talk* Words**

encourage	_____
environment	_____
government	_____
improve	_____
native	_____
subway	_____
teleportation	_____
world	_____
_____	_____

Usage

Match the vocabulary words to the pictures on the following two pages. Then write the words next to the pictures. List words below that do not match a picture. Do you know what they mean? Have people in your group help you understand the words you don't know.

_____   _____   _____   _____

_____   _____   _____   _____

Let's Start

Work in small groups. Ask other students what they *can or can't, might or might not, will or won't* use to travel. Complete each sentence with the name of someone in your group.

Example: *Who can drive a car? Maria can drive a car.*

Ask questions. Write a student's name.

1. _____ might take the bus to school tomorrow.

2. _____ won't buy a new car.

3. _____ might not carpool to work.

4. _____ will travel to another country this year.

Now ask other students about travel situations or activities they *can or can't, might or might not, will or won't* do. Use the following ideas. Add others.

Travel: *How will you get to school tomorrow? I'll drive.*
Languages: *What languages can you speak? I can speak Italian and French.*

Let's Talk...

1. Name at least eight kinds of transportation.

2. What kind of transportation do you use the most? Why?

3. What kinds of transportation did your native country have ten years ago?

4. What kind of transportation did *you* use then? Why?

5. Have you ridden in a subway? On a plane? In a train? On a bus? Talk about your experiences.

6. Have you driven a bus? A train? Flown a plane? Talk about it.

7. When have you carpooled? Who was in the car with you? Where did you go?

8. What can the government do to encourage people to carpool more? Explain.

9. What country do you think has an excellent transportation system? Why?

10. How do you think we can improve today's transportation systems?

11. Imagine what the world will be like in twenty years. What kinds of transportation do you think we might have?

12. What is teleportation? Do you think that it will be a popular transportation system in the future? Why or why not?

A. Survey

Interview students in your class. How do they get to school? Fill in the chart.

Student's name	How do you get to school?	What main streets do you live near?	What time do you leave for school?	Can you drive?

How will you get to school tomorrow? Can you carpool with someone?
(You might ride to your next class meeting with a new friend!)

B. Fill in

Work in a small group. Write the names of the automobile manufacturers and airline companies for each country. Then discuss what you think about them.

Italy _____   Germany _____   Korea _____   United States _____

Japan _____   England _____   Sweden _____   your country _____

C. Draw

In your group invent the perfect transportation system. Make it inexpensive, fast, and safe for the environment. Draw a picture of it below. Explain to the class how it works.

Lesson 5

Pets

Vocabulary New Words

animal	most
bullfight	neglect
chicken fight	part of
definition	people
dictionary	pet
dog race	shelter
ever	such as
human	unusual

Let's Talk Words

abuse	take care of
animal rights group	treat
buy	_____
dislike	_____
feel	_____
find	_____
grow up	_____
guess	

Usage

Work with a partner. Read the questions in the *Let's talk* section. Circle the vocabulary words for this lesson and guess their meanings. If necessary, use your dictionary. Then discuss your vocabulary definitions with the class.

Let's Start

Divide the class into two teams. One team member chooses a team player and asks a student a question beginning with "Have you ever...?" If the student answers "yes," members of the other team can ask three information questions such as, "When?", "Where?", and "With whom?" Each team can continue until a student answers "no." Then the other team asks questions. Verbs can't be used more than once. Write some questions below.

Student 1 team A:	*Have you ever bought a pet in a pet store?*
Student 2 team A:	*Yes.*
Student 1 team B:	*What kind of pet?*
Student 2 team A:	*A dog.*
Student 2 team B:	*When did you buy it?*
Student 2 team A:	*Last month.*
Student 3 team B:	*I don't have a question.*

Have you ever _____?

Have you ever _____?

Have you ever _____?

Let's Talk...

1. What are five popular pets people have?

2. How did people treat pets in the city where you grew up?

3. Have you ever had a pet? Talk about it.

4. Why do people have pets? Why do some people dislike pets?

5. Did you find your pet, get it from a shelter, or buy it in a store? Explain.

6. What are some unusual pets that you have seen in your native country?

7. What are some other unusual pets people have in countries that you have lived in or visited?

8. What do you think about people who believe pets are part of their family? Have you ever had a pet that you felt was part of your family?

9. Do you think that humans are more important than animals? Why or why not?

10. The United States has animal rights groups (groups that protect animals from abuse and neglect). Does your country have animal rights groups? What do you think about animal rights groups?

11. Does your country have sporting events that use animals (chicken fights, horse races, bullfights, dog races, or horse tripping)? Have you ever gone to one of those events? What do you think about them?

A. Survey

Find out who the pet lovers are in your class by completing the chart below.

Student's name	Kind of pet	Name of pet	Where the student got it

What are the most popular pets students in your class have? Are they the most popular pets in your native country?

B. Think

Write the names of as many kinds of animals as you can. Look in your dictionary to find names of unusual animals. Circle the most popular animals that people have as pets.

_____   _____   _____   _____

_____   _____   _____   _____

C. Write

Look at the words that you circled above. Have you ever had any of these animals as a pet? Which ones? Write a little bit about a pet you have or have had.

_____

_____

_____

D. Draw

In your notebook draw and fill in an identification (ID) tag for a pet that you have or have had. Write the pet's name, your name, your address, and your telephone number.

Lesson 6 — Job Interviews

Vocabulary — New Words

job skill	prepare
interview	ask
employer	hire
characteristic	fire
company	get
question	look for
employment	file
alphabetically	answer

Let's Talk Words

application	last
best way	network
duty	possible
experience	reference
expression	reliable
guide	salary
hiring practices	state
important	supervisor

Usage

Filing is one important job skill. There are many ways to file. Some companies file alphabetically. Practice filing by alphabetizing your new vocabulary words.

1. _alphabetically_
2. _____
3. _____
4. _____
5. _____
6. _____
7. _____
8. _____
9. _____
10. _____
11. _____
12. _____
13. _____
14. _____
15. _____
16. _____

Let's Start

Discuss other job skills. List them below.

1. *Working well with others is an important job skill.*
2. _____
3. _____
4. _____
5. _____

Now practice a job interview with a partner. First think about questions that employers ask, and write a list together on a separate piece of paper. Then take turns interviewing each other. Give each other ideas on how to improve interviewing skills.

Let's Talk...

1. Getting a new job can be difficult. Name at least four ways people find jobs. Example – *Networking is a good way to find a job.*

2. Name five things that people do to prepare for job interviews.

3. What are five questions that employers often ask at job interviews?

4. Give five or more answers to your questions.

5. When an employer asks you if you have any questions, what do you answer? State five possible questions you can ask about the job or the company.

6. Think about your last job interview. Tell about your experience. What questions did the employer ask you?

7. Did you get the job at your last interview? Why do you think the employer did or didn't hire you?

8. What has been the best way for you to find a job? Talk about how you have looked for work.

9. What do you think are some important characteristics employers look for when they are hiring people? Examples – *A person who comes to work on time. A reliable person.*

10. Do you think that hiring practices are fair? Why or why not?

11. Why do employers fire some people? Name five reasons.

12. "Working your way to the top" is a popular expression in English. What do you think it means?

A. Fill in

Fill out the job application.

Name_____
          Last   First   Middle

Address _____
          Street   City   State   Zip Code

Phone Number ( )_____ Are you over 18?_____ Date available_____

Circle the last grade you completed   5 6 7 8 9 10 11 12   college   university

List your employment skills_____

List your work experience. Start with your last or current employer first. If you need more space, attach another paper.

Employer (Company) _____

Supervisor's name _____ Phone number ( )_____

Your title _____ Job duties:_____ Salary _____

Dates of employment: from _____ to _____   May we contact employer? _____

Reason for leaving?_____

List two references who have known you for at least one year. Write their names and telephone numbers.

_____

_____

Date _____ Applicant's signature _____

Write in the hours you are able to work under the days. Write A.M. or P.M.

	Monday	Tuesday	Wednesday	Thursday	Friday	Saturday	Sunday
Day							
Night							

B. Discuss

Filling out a job application correctly is important. Talk about your job application with a partner. Then talk about your partner's. Help each other.

Lesson 7 The Best of Everything

Vocabulary New Words

active	nice
attractive	noisiest
best	quietest
everything	sell
explain	shortest
friendliest	talkative
happiest	tallest
history (of)	variety (of)

Let's Talk Words

ago	newspaper
choice	reviewer
choose	saddest
contest	shop
embarrass	winner
frustrate	worst
local	_____
magazine	_____

Usage

Antonym means opposite. Write the vocabulary words that are the antonyms of the words below.

1. tallest _____
2. same_____
3. future_____
4. lazy_____

5. now _____
6. buy_____
7. noisiest_____
8. happiest_____

9. mean, bad_____
10. ugly_____
11. best_____
12. listen_____

Let's Start

Work with a partner. Look around your class. Choose a student who matches the description below. Write that student's name in the space.

1. The happiest student is _____.

2. The most active student is_____.

3. The most talkative student is_____.

4. The friendliest student is _____.

5. The quietest student is_____.

6. The tallest student is_____.

7. The shortest student is_____.

8. The most attractive student is_____.

Let's Talk...

1. What's the best city to visit in your country? Why?

2. What's the most popular TV show in your country? What's it about?

3. What's the best newspaper in your country? Why is it the best?

4. What's the most popular magazine in your country? What's it about?

5. Who was the most important person in your country ten years ago? Why was that person so important?

6. Who was the most important person in the history of your country? What did that person do? Who is the most important person now?

7. What do you think was the best restaurant in your country five years ago? What about now?

8. What is the most popular sport in your country? What do you think is the most popular sport in the world? Why do you think that sport is so popular?

9. Which car do you think was the most popular last year? What about this year?

10. Think about all the department stores in which you have shopped. Which one was the best? Why? What does it sell?

11. What was the most interesting place you have ever visited? Talk about it.

12. What's the best thing about where you live now? Why?

...eviewer for a local newspaper. You have gone many places and done many ...se the winners for the "Best of Everything" contest for your city. Discuss your choices in a group.

The Best of Everything

The best of everything for the city of _____ by _____.

The best restaurant is _____ because _____.

The best auto repair place is _____ because _____.

The best hair salon is _____ because _____.

The best supermarket is _____ because _____.

The best park is _____ because _____.

The best school is _____ because _____.

The best bank is _____ because _____.

The best fast food place is _____ because _____.

The best shopping mall is _____ because _____.

The best movie is _____ because _____.

The best TV show is _____ because _____.

The best department store is _____ because _____.

The best newspaper is _____ because _____.

The best magazine is _____ because _____.

The best TV channel is _____ because _____.

The best teacher is _____ because _____.

Over all, the best thing in my city is _____ because _____.

The worst thing about my city is _____ because _____.

B. Write

Write about the following topics. Share your experiences with a student.

1. The happiest day in your life
2. The saddest day in your life
3. The most embarrassing day in your life
4. The most frustrating day in your life

Lesson 8

Family

Vocabulary New Words

aunt	male
brother	mother
children	nephew
daughter	niece
family	parent
family tree	relative
father	sibling
female	sister
grandfather	son
grandmother	spouse
grandparent	uncle
husband	wife

Let's Talk Words

a lot	perfect
approach	related to
argue	teach
avoid	together
childhood	_____
cousin	_____
describe	_____
generous	_____
get along with	_____
in-law	_____
member	_____
occupation	_____

Usage Think about your family. Then complete the chart using the vocabulary words.

Female relative	Her name	Male relative	His name	Word for both relatives
wife	*Sue*	*husband*	*John*	*spouse*
sister				
mother				
aunt				
daughter				
grandmother				
niece				

Let's Start Draw a family picture. Identify the people and their relationships to you.

(empty box)

Now draw a family tree in your notebook. Write in family members' names. Talk about your family with someone in your class.

Let's Talk...

1. What family members do you live with at the present time? How are they related to you? What are their occupations?

2. Do you have siblings? How many brothers do you have? How many sisters? Where do they live? What are they doing now?

3. Which family member do you get along with the best? Why?

4. Who do you argue with a lot? Are you arguing with that person now? What are you arguing about?

5. Are you married? If so, when did you get married? What were you doing when your spouse asked you, or you asked your spouse, to marry? If you are not married, do you want to get married? What are you doing to approach or avoid marriage?

6. Do you have children? If so, how many children do you have? Talk about them.

If you don't have children, do you want to have children? Why or why not?

7. Which aunts, uncles, cousins, or relatives did you see a lot when you were a child? What did you do together?

8. Which relatives do you call? Did you call a relative last week? Which one? What did you talk about?

9. Think about an older relative. Who are you thinking about? What did that relative teach you?

10. What family member do you want to see that you haven't seen in a long time? Why do you want to see that person? Why haven't you seen that person in a long time?

11. Do you think that families you see on TV or in the movies are like families in your country? Why or why not? Are they like American families? Explain.

12. Describe a perfect family.

A. Survey

Ask a few students about their families. Complete the chart. Then share the information with other students.

Name	Siblings' names	Where do they live?	How many children do you have?	Favorite relative

Do many students in class have children? Brothers and sisters? The same favorite relative? Who has the largest family? The smallest?

B. Think

How would you describe your relatives? Complete the chart with family members' names. Then tell a partner why each relative matches the definition you chose.

Adjective	Name	Relationship	Why?
honest	Marvin	Father	He does what he promises.
happy			
depressed			
shy			
generous			

C. Discuss

Form into groups. Show pictures of your family to your group. Talk about what the people were doing in the picture, and what the people are doing now.

D. Write

In your notebook write a story about the best day in your childhood. What were you doing? What relatives were you with? Share your story with the class.

Lesson 9

Gender Roles

Vocabulary New Words

gender
get paid (for)
go (out)
home
accomplishment   household
change   leadership
chore   look up to
congratulate   make
date   marriage

men   usually
nowadays who
outside   whom
past   women
respect   work
role
society
traditionally
typically

Let's Talk Words

expect   traditional
house   typical
laundry   women's rights
modern   movement
put (away)   _____
put (out)   _____
take (out)   _____
   trash   _____

Usage

Find and circle your new vocabulary words in the story. Then read the story with another student. Help each other understand your new words.

In society gender roles are changing. Traditionally, men asked women to go out on dates. After marriage, men usually worked outside the home. Women typically stayed home to take care of their children and do household chores. Nowadays, almost as many women as men work outside the home. The women get paid for their work, and their employers often congratulate them for their accomplishments.
In the past, society only looked up to and respected men, but now women are more active in leadership roles.

Let's Start

When your teacher reads the questions, shout out, "men," "women," or "both." Then discuss why you chose that answer.

Who pays on a date? Who calls whom for the date?

Who gives the first kiss? Who changes the babies' diapers?

Who asks whom to dance? Who asks whom to marry?

Who opens the door for whom? Who cleans the house?

Can you think of other situations? Ask the class.

Let's Talk...

1. What are five jobs men usually do in your country? What are five jobs women usually do in your country?

2. In your home who usually takes out the trash, puts away the laundry, takes care of the children, cleans the house? Why?

3. In your country does a man call a woman for a date or does a woman call a man? Why?

4. What's a man's role in your country? (*What does society expect him to do?*) What's a woman's role in your country? (*What does society expect her to do?*)

5. Do you think traditional roles for men and women are easier than modern roles? Why or why not?

6. What was a typical "woman's" job fifty years ago? What was a typical "man's" job fifty years ago?

7. Do men and women always get equal pay for the same job in your country? Explain.

8. Do you think that most people look up to men or to women for leadership? Why?

9. Do you know which countries have "women's rights movements"? Name them. Is there a "women's rights movement" in your country? Why or why not?

10. Do you think that the women's rights movement has helped women? Men? Society in general? Explain your answers.

11. How do you feel about a "men's rights group"? Why?

12. What has been the greatest accomplishment a woman has made in your country? Who was she? What did she do?

A. Survey

Work in groups. Interview the members of your group. Ask them about their roles at home and in society.

Student's name	What chores do you do?	What kind of work do you do outside the home?	What are your accomplishments?

Do men do certain household chores? Do women? Look at your chart and decide.

B. Fill in

Some gifts are most popular with women. Other gifts are most popular with men. Some gifts are popular with both men and women. Complete the chart using the following words. Add words of your own. Compare your list with other students in your class.

dress	cuff links	nail polish	_____
aftershave	perfume	lipstick	_____
purse	wallet	panty hose	_____
razor	skirt	makeup	_____
computer	wrench	nose hair clippers	_____

Men's gifts	Women's gifts	Men's and women's gifts

C. Write

What are some roles that men and women have in this country? How are they changing? What will they be like in ten years? Write your answers in your notebook.

Lesson 10

Vocabulary  New Words

holiday
interesting
pay
place
reason
special
young

celebrate
cover
dictate

Let's Talk Words

Dr. Martin Luther
   King, Jr. Day
Father's Day
Halloween
Independence Day
lonely
Memorial Day
Mother's Day

New Year's Day
tell
Thanksgiving
Valentine's Day
Veteran's Day
Washington's
   Birthday
work

Usage

Work in pairs. Cover your partner's *new* vocabulary words. Dictate the new vocabulary words out of order to your partner. Your partner will write them below. Check your partner's work. Then your partner will dictate to you. Discuss the meanings of any words you don't know.

_____   _____   _____

_____   _____   _____

_____   _____

_____   _____

Let's Start

Where are the students in your class from? Write the names of the cities in the chart below. Ask the students from different backgrounds to tell you the names of major holidays they celebrate. Find out when people celebrate these holidays, how they celebrate them, and why. Discuss your chart with the class.

Cities	Holidays	When celebrated?	How?	Why?

Let's Talk...

1. What are three holidays that many people celebrate around the world? Talk about them.

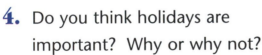

2. Name three holidays you think are the most important in your country. Why are they important? How do you celebrate them?

3. Talk about holiday food. What special kinds of food do people eat on important holidays in your country? What do people drink on these holidays?

4. Do you think holidays are important? Why or why not?

5. When you were a child, what holiday did you like best? Why?

6. Did you dislike any holidays when you were very young? Which ones and why?

7. What holidays do you like best now? Why?

8. What holidays have you celebrated recently? How did you celebrate them? With whom did you celebrate?

9. What day do you want to celebrate as a holiday? Why?

10. Think about places where you have worked. Were people paid for holidays when they stayed home from work? Why or why not? Which holidays were they usually paid for, if any?

11. Holiday time can be lonely for some people. What can you do to help lonely people during holiday seasons?

A. Think

What do you know about the United States? In which months do these holidays occur? How do people celebrate? What is the reason for these holidays? Work in small groups to complete the chart.

Holiday	Month	How people celebrate	Reason for celebrating
Thanksgiving			
Halloween			
Independence Day			
Memorial Day			
Dr. Martin Luther King, Jr. Day			
Washington's Birthday			
Veteran's Day			
Mother's Day			
Father's Day			
Valentine's Day			
New Year's Day			

Discuss as a class which other holidays students also celebrate in their native countries.

B. Fill in

Complete the sentences. Then discuss with a partner.

1. The happiest holiday is _____ because _____.

2. The most interesting holiday is _____ because _____.

3. The liveliest holiday is _____ because _____.

4. The worst holiday is _____ because _____.

5. The best holiday is _____ because _____.

C. Write

Write about your favorite holiday in your notebook. When do you celebrate? How? Why?

Lesson 11

Superstitions

Vocabulary New Words

catch
four-leaf clover
good luck
horseshoe
ladder
lucky
mirror
open
rabbit's foot

salt
spill
superstition
sweep
true
umbrella
under
walk
wedding

bad luck
believe
black cat
bouquet
break

Let's Talk Words

get married   _____
happen   _____
invent   _____
say   _____
secret   _____
unlucky   _____
unmarried   _____

_____   _____

_____   _____

Usage

Work in a group. Write a story that describes all the pictures in this lesson using as many vocabulary words as you can.

_____

_____

_____

_____

_____

Let's Start

Work with a partner. Discuss whether or not you believe in these superstitions. Then write "good luck" or "bad luck."

1. shoes on a table _____

2. horseshoe _____

3. rabbit's foot_____

4. broken mirror _____

5. opening an umbrella in a room
   _____

6. four-leaf clover _____

7. spilling salt _____

8. walking under a ladder _____

9. black cat _____

10. catching a bouquet at a
    wedding_____

Let's Talk...

1. Some people in the United States think a four-leaf clover is "lucky." What do you think are five lucky things in your country?

2. Many people in the United States believe if you walk under a ladder, you will have bad luck. What are five things people in your country believe bring bad luck?

3. What might happen if you break a mirror, spill salt, or sweep an unmarried woman's feet?

4. What might happen if you put shoes on a table, let a black cat walk in front of you, or open an umbrella in a house?

5. Are there any superstitions in your country? Name five.

6. Who told you about the superstitions that you know? What did that person say?

7. Some people in the United States think the number "7" is a lucky number. They think this number will help them win money. What number is lucky in your country? Why?

8. Some people in the United States believe when the 13th day of the month is on a Friday it is an unlucky day. What numbers bring bad luck in your country? Are there any days, months, or years that are unlucky in your country? Discuss.

9. Do you believe in superstitions? Why or why not?

10. Have you ever had a superstition come true? Tell about your experience.

A. Survey

What can these superstitions mean? Who told you about them? Invent answers.
Then discuss your ideas with another student.

If you...	What might or will happen?	Who told you about it?	What did he or she say?
break a mirror	*You'll have 7 years of bad luck.*	*my grandmother*	*She said, "If you break a mirror you'll have 7 years of bad luck."*
walk under a ladder			
put shoes on a table			
open an umbrella in the house			
spill salt			
find a four-leaf clover			

B. Fill in

What were some secrets you told family members?

Whom did you tell?	What did you say?
I told my sister I caught the wedding bouquet.	*I said, "I might get married soon."*

C. Write

Answer these questions. Then ask other students what they wrote.

What do you say when someone tells you about their bad luck?_____

_____

What can you tell someone about your good or bad luck? _____

_____

Lesson 12

Sleep

Vocabulary New Words

always
blanket
daily
day off
dream

get (up)
go (to bed)
good night
hour
lullaby
never
nightmare
often
position
rarely

schedule
sleep
sleeping aid
sleepwalk
snore
sometimes
tired
tuck in

Let's Talk Words

alarm clock
allow
enough
noise
oversleep
ring
scream
sing
sound

wake up
_____
_____
_____
_____
_____
_____
_____
_____

Usage

Work with a partner. Read your vocabulary words to each other. Decide together where you think the words belong. Then complete the chart.

Schedule		Sleep	
daily		lullaby	

Let's Start

How often do you do these things? Write *always, usually, sometimes, rarely,* or *never.*

I _____ get up early.
I _____ use a blanket.
I _____ have a nightmare.
I _____ snore.
I _____ sleep at the movies.
I _____ sleep on the beach.
I _____ sleep on the sofa.

I _____ go to bed late.
I _____ use sleeping aids.
I _____ dream.
I _____ walk in my sleep.
I _____ sleep in the park.
I _____ sleep in front of the TV.
I _____ sleep on the floor.

Work in small groups. Talk about your sleeping habits. Ask other students about theirs.

Student A: *I always get up early. How about you?*
Student B: *I never get up early.*
Student A: *Why?*
Student B: *I work at night, and I'm tired in the morning.*

Let's Talk...

1. What is your daily sleep schedule? How many hours of sleep do you usually get? Do you get enough sleep? Why or why not?

2. What position do you usually sleep in? How often do you sleep in that position?

3. Name ten or more places where people sleep. What unusual place have you slept in? How often do you sleep there?

4. When you can't sleep, what kinds of things do you do? Do you drink hot tea? How often do you do those things?

5. What are some unusual things people do in their sleep (scream, sleepwalk)? Name three more. What unusual things do you do in your sleep? How often do you do them? How do you know?

6. There are people in United States who allow their pets to sleep in bed with them. Do people in your country do that? What about you?

7. What wakes you up in the morning? Do you have an alarm clock? Have you ever overslept because you didn't hear your alarm clock ring? What happened?

8. What time did you usually go to bed when you were a child? How did you feel about going to bed at that time? What special things did your parents do for you before you went to bed? Did they sing a lullaby to you, tuck you in, and say good night?

9. Talk about a good dream that you have had recently.

10. Talk about a nightmare that you have had recently.

11. Do you believe that dreams come true? Why or why not?

A. Survey

Find a student who has done one of the following bedtime activities. Write the student's name in the space. Then ask the student, "How often?" Write *always*, *usually*, *sometimes*, *rarely*, or *never*.

Student's name	How often	Bedtime activity
		listens to music in bed.
		uses sleeping aids.
		sleeps with a house pet.
		walks in his or her sleep.
		has nightmares.
		wakes up screaming.
		snores.

What bedtime activities do the students do most often? What do they rarely do?

B. Fill in

Unscramble these words and phrases. Then use each one in a sentence.

1. laulybl _____ _____

2. rmaethnig _____ _____

3. nogodhtgi _____ _____

4. raedm _____ _____

5. kwlaspele _____ _____

6. debogot _____ _____

C. Write

Write about a dream or nightmare that you have had. Read it to the class.

_____

_____

_____

Lesson 13   Stealing

Vocabulary

New Words

age	less
chronically	person
common	punishment
fewer	someone
frequently	steal
	thief

Let's Talk Words

criminal	victim
future	violent
hide	_____
judge	_____
rob	_____
robbery	_____

Usage

Game: Guess your vocabulary words... Work in groups of four. Form into two teams by choosing a partner in your group. *Player 1* in each team will pick the words, and *Player 2* will guess the words.

How to play:

1. Write all the vocabulary words on small pieces of paper and put them in a bag.
2. **Team A:** *Player 1* picks a word (*thief*) and shows it to *Player 1* on **Team B**.
3. **Team B:** *Player 1* gives a clue for that word (*a person who takes something that doesn't belong to him*) to *Player 2* on **Team B**. If he guesses incorrectly, *Player 1* on **Team A** can ask *Player 2* on **Team A**.
4. The teams take turns choosing words and giving clues.
5. The team that guesses the most words wins.

Let's Start

Work with a partner. Decide what thieves steal from each place. Write the item(s). Then write *less* or *fewer* to show what happens after the thieves have been to each place. Discuss your answers as a class.

Place	Item	After the thief has been there...		
bank	_money_	the bank has	*less*	*money* .
library	_____	the library has	_____	_____ .
restaurant	_____	the restaurant has	_____	_____ .
hotel	_____	the hotel has	_____	_____ .
post office	_____	the post office has	_____	_____ .
office	_____	the office has	_____	_____ .
farm	_____	the farm has	_____	_____ .

Let's Talk...

1. Where do most criminals steal from? Name five places.

2. What are five common things thieves steal?

3. Where do you think thieves might look first when they enter a house? Where can you hide things in your house so a thief won't find them?

4. In your country, what's the punishment for stealing?

5. What are the ages of most thieves in your country? How about in other countries around the world?

6. Talk about a time when a thief stole something from you. What happened? How did you feel? What did you do?

7. How have thieves changed in the past five years? Are they more or less violent? Are they older or younger? Why do you think that?

8. Do you think there will be more or less crime in the future? Why?

9. How can a person avoid becoming a victim of robbery?

10. Why do you think people steal? Give three reasons.

11. What can we do to people who frequently steal things? How can we stop them from stealing?

12. You are a judge. What punishment do you give for stealing? Why?

A. Survey

Thieves have stolen things from almost everyone. Ask students what thieves have stolen from them. Fill in the chart.

Name	What the thief stole	When	Where	Do you have less or fewer of what the thief stole?

Where do most robberies happen? What is the most common thing thieves steal?

B. Fill in

Here are some common items that thieves steal. After they steal the items, are there less or *fewer* of them? Write *less* or *fewer* in the space.

1. _____ jewelry
2. _____ art
3. _____ computers
4. _____ TVs
5. _____ money

6. _____ telephones
7. _____ pianos
8. _____ music
9. _____ coins
10. _____ dogs

11. _____ earrings
12. _____ diamonds
13. _____ furniture
14. _____ cats
15. _____ necklaces

C. Write

Think about question **6** in the *Let's Talk* section. Write about a time when a thief stole something that you had. When did this happen? What did the thief take? What did you do about it?

_____

_____

_____

_____

Lesson 14   Gossip

Vocabulary New Words

article	loud
continue	news
false	recently
fill	spread
gossip	whisper
hear	wrong

Let's Talk Words

right   _____

_____ _____

_____ _____

_____ _____

_____ _____

_____ _____

Usage

Work in pairs. Read the vocabulary words to each other. Then complete the sentences.

1. I like to watch the _____ on television.

2. Most gossip is _____.

3. I like people. I don't like to _____ gossip about them.

4. When people gossip they usually_____ so no one will _____ them.

5. My parents told me it was _____to gossip.

6. I dislike writers who _____ their _____with gossip.

Now write your own sentences using some of your vocabulary words.

_____

_____

_____

Let's Start

Spreading gossip. In your notebook, write five sentences about something unusual that has happened to you. Don't show anyone.

The teacher will choose a student. That student will whisper to another student what he or she wrote. The student who hears the gossip will whisper it to another student. This will continue until the last student says the sentences out loud. Then the student who wrote the sentences will read them. Everyone will see how gossip spreads and how stories change. (As you spread the gossip, say the name of the person who told *you*.)

Now tell the class about some gossip you have heard recently at work, home, or on the phone. Remember to tell the class who told you.

Let's Talk...

1. What are five things people usually gossip about?

2. Where can a person hear gossip? Name five places.

3. Which magazines are filled with gossip? Name them.

4. What do you think people said about you when you told them you were going to study English?

5. When was the last time you heard gossip from a friend or family member? Tell your group about it.

6. What gossip have you heard on the news recently?

7. Have you ever spread gossip? If yes, what did you say? If not, why didn't you?

8. Who gossips more, men or women? Why do you think that?

9. Why do you think people gossip?

10. Do you think most gossip is true or false? Why? Do you think that it is right or wrong to gossip? Why?

A. Fill In

How do people spread gossip? Add the missing vowels. Then work with a partner, and add your own ideas.

1. m __ __ t h
2. t __ l __ p h __ n __
3. n __ w s p __ p __ r
4. m __ g __ z __ n __

5. r __ d __ __
6. l __ t t __ r
7. n __ t __
8. t __ l __ v __ s __ __ n

9. f r __ __ n d   _____
10. w h __ s p __ r   _____
11. b __ __ k   _____
12. t __ l k   _____

B. Write

Spreading gossip

Talk to the students in your class. Ask them to tell you some gossip about famous people. Write the gossip you have heard and who told you.

an employer: _____supervisor_____

    gossip: _____*My friend **told** me his supervisor was always late for work.*_____

           _____*My friend **said** his supervisor was always late for work.*_____

1. **an actress:**_____

    gossip: _____

_____

2. **an actor:**_____

    gossip: _____

_____

3. **an athlete:**_____

    gossip: _____

_____

4. **a singer:**_____

    gossip: _____

_____

C. Discuss

In small groups discuss what students say about their teachers.

Lesson 15 Ghosts and the Supernatural

Vocabulary New Words

careful	investigate	séance
create	know	search
creature	leave (behind)	should
Earth	look (like)	space ship
event	mysterious	strange
exist	phenomena	supernatural
free	phenomenon	UFO
ghost	planet	understand
imagine	present	witness

Let's Talk Words

eye witness
hold (a séance)
legal
make contact (with)
spend
take (place)
_____
_____
_____

Usage

Work with a partner. Discuss the vocabulary words you know.
Use your dictionary to help you understand the words you don't know.
Then match the words in each column.

_____e_____ 1. séance		a. investigate
_____ 2. planet		b. phenomenon
_____ 3. ghost		c. know
_____ 4. understand		d. Earth
_____ 5. mysterious		e. event
_____ 6. UFO		f. supernatural
_____ 7. search		g. strange

Let's Start

Your teacher will read the following questions. Raise your hand if your answer is yes. Write the name of a student who has also answered yes. Ask that student about his or her experience.

1. Have you ever witnessed a UFO? _____
2. Have you ever gone to a séance? _____
3. Do you believe creatures live on other planets? _____
4. Do you think that supernatural phenomena exist? _____

Work in a group. Imagine a space ship has left behind a very strange and mysterious creature. What does it look like? How should you greet it? How should you treat it? What should you do with it? What should you feed it? Should you let it go free? (*You should study it carefully!*)

Work with your group to create a picture and a story about your mysterious creature. Present your project to the class.

Let's Talk...

1. What are ghosts? Do you believe they exist? Why or why not? Explain.

2. Where do people usually see ghosts? Have you ever seen a ghost? Discuss.

3. Do you believe that UFOs or creatures from other planets exist? Why or why not?

4. Where do people usually see a UFO? Has anyone you've known seen a UFO? Have you? Talk about it.

5. Do you think the government should spend money to investigate or search for UFOs? Why or why not?

6. Has any mysterious or supernatural event taken place in your country? Explain.

7. Have you ever been to a séance? Do you know anyone who has? Talk about your experience.

8. Is it legal to hold a séance in your country? Do you think it should be? Why or why not?

9. Imagine you are an "eye witness" to a ghost, a UFO, or a supernatural phenomenon. What should you do? Should you tell your friends and family? Should you call the police? Will people believe you? Discuss.

A. Think

Imagine you are a young child. A ghost of your mother or father is watching you and telling you what you should and shouldn't do. What is the ghost saying?

You should	You shouldn't
You should do your homework.	*You shouldn't eat too much candy.*

Discuss your lists with other students in your class.

B. Role Play

Work in pairs. Imagine you are at a séance. Who do you want to make contact with and talk to? Your partner will become that person. Tell your partner about three problems you have. Ask your partner what you should do about them. Your partner (acting as the person you have chosen) should be able to answer your questions.

My partner is _____.

What should I do about _____?

What should I do about _____?

What should I do about _____?

C. Write

Do you believe in ghosts? Why or why not. Explain your answer in four sentences.

_____

_____

_____

_____

Lesson 16   Love

Vocabulary New Words

appropriate	lazy
boyfriend	love
break up	relationship
consider	sloppy
difficult	teenager
girlfriend	would
impolite	

Let's Talk Words

approve	generation
bring home	judge
care about	potential
constant	race
culture	religion
decide	_____
disapprove	_____

Usage

Work with a partner. Read all the vocabulary words to each other. Decide which words describe people and which describe their feelings.

People		Feelings	
race		approve	

Let's Start

Work in pairs. Read the situation below. Decide who will play the role of the teenager and who will play the role of the parent. If you were the parent, what would you do? If you were the teenager, what would you do? Role play.

PARENT: You know your teenager is in a difficult relationship. Your child is dating someone who is sloppy, lazy, and impolite. You want them to break up. Talk to your teenager and try to get him or her to consider dating another person.

TEENAGER: You are in love! You think the person you are dating is the best thing that has ever happened to you. You see this person as wonderful, fun to be with, and attractive. You think your family doesn't understand your relationship. Explain your situation and feelings.

Let's Talk...

1. What five characteristics do young people usually consider when they look for a boyfriend or a girlfriend?

2. How do older people, or the parents of the younger generation, usually judge a potential partner? How do these characteristics differ from the younger generation's ideas of a potential partner?

3. Did your parents disapprove of any of your past relationships? Why?

4. Did you disapprove of any of your children's or sibling's relationships? Explain why.

5. If you disapproved of a family member's relationship, would you tell that person how you felt? Why or why not?

6. Have you ever dated someone whom you would never want to bring home to your family? If so, explain why you chose not to introduce that person to your family. If not, did you always introduce your dates to your family? Explain.

7. Would you break up with someone if your family disapproved of that person? Why or why not? Have you ever broken up with someone because of that reason? Why or why not?

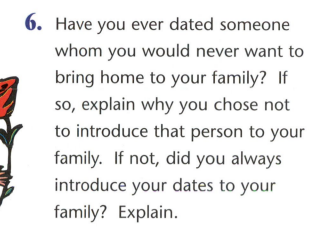

8. In your country, who decides whom a person should marry? Does the person decide, or the parents? How do you feel about that?

9. How do you feel about people who don't marry someone of the same race, religion, or culture? Why? If that person were someone in your family, would you feel differently? Explain.

A. Think

(If you aren't single, imagine you are.)
Form into small groups to discuss how you should handle these difficult situations.

What would you do...

What would you do if you loved someone, but that person didn't love you?
(Imagine that you were always thinking about that person.)

_____

_____

What would you do if someone loved you, but you didn't love that person?
(Imagine that person constantly called you and kept asking to see you.)

_____

_____

B. Fill In

Who loves you? Who do you love? Complete the chart. Share your list with a partner.

Loves me		I love	
Name	Relationship to me	Name	Relationship to me

C. Write

Write a love letter to someone you care about—husband, wife, boyfriend, or girlfriend.
Explain how you feel and why.

_____

_____

_____

_____

Vocabulary New Words

associate
employee
less than
manage
million

more than
owe
raise
shout
sight
stress

Let's Talk Words

afraid	negative	relax
better	nervous	responsibility
cause	occur	scare
combat	optimist	throughout
deal with	pessimist	upset
destroy	physical	way
handle	positive	_____
mental	reduce	_____

Usage

Word Association Game Work in pairs. One student will say a word. The other student will choose a word that can be associated with that word and then explain why. Write your word pairs below.

Student 1: *upset*
Student 2: *stress*
Student 2: *People feel upset when they have a lot of stress in their lives.*

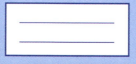

upset
stress

Let's Start

Compare the situations and decide which would be more or less stressful. Write *more* or *less*. Then form into groups and discuss your ideas.

1. raising two children _____ stressful <u>than</u> managing a hundred employees

2. owing the government a million dollars _____ stressful <u>than</u> being sick for a year

3. losing your sight _____ stressful <u>than</u> losing your hearing

4. having too much to do _____ stressful <u>than</u> having nothing to do

5. your boss shouting at you _____ stressful <u>than</u> your spouse shouting at you

Let's Talk...

1. What is stress? What five things can cause stress?

2. What are five positive ways people deal with stress?

3. What are five negative ways people deal with stress?

4. Talk about the most stressful day that you have ever had. How did you handle the stress?

5. When you were a child, how did people in your family deal with stress? Give some examples.

6. Have you ever broken or destroyed anything when you felt very stressed? What have you done to combat stress?

7. When someone you know is very upset and shows signs of stress, does it scare you? What do you think might happen? Has this ever happened to you? Explain.

8. Would you take a very stressful job if you were paid a high salary? Why or why not?

9. How can people reduce stress in their lives? What are some things people do to relax?

10. Where do you think it is most stressful to live? Why?

11. Do you think that being single is less stressful then being married? Why or why not?

12. Do you think it is more stressful to work at a job that is physically or mentally challenging? Why?

13. Are you an optimist or a pessimist? Why is it better to be an optimist when negative events occur in your life?

A. Puzzle

Complete the crossword puzzle using words that show what people do to *relieve stress*.

Across

5. Yell, scream, or_____ .

6. _____ a magazine.

8. Take a long, quiet _____ with a friend.

Down

1. _____ to music.

2. Take a long hot _____ .

3. _____ healthy foods.

4. Lift weights and _____ .

7. _____ on the telephone.

B. Think

Throughout life people have stress. Compare your life now to your life when you were a child. What is more stressful now? What is less stressful? Why? Discuss in a group.

Sample situations:

Budgeting my money is more stressful now than when I was a child because I have bills that I need to pay.

Staying out late at night is less stressful now than when I was a child because I don't have to be home when my parents tell me to.

Vocabulary New Words

immediate family
issue
move out
remain

Let's Talk Words

across	regret
adult children	_____
advice	_____
down	_____
on your own	_____
over	_____
reaction	_____

Usage

Work with a partner. Each of you will choose a picture on the following two pages and write a short story about it using your vocabulary words. Share your stories and guess your partner's picture. Then use your vocabulary words to talk about the remaining pictures.

Let's Start

Think about your immediate family. What are some things you have told your children to do or not to do? Did they ever listen? What did they say? Did you ever tell them to move out? What issues made you think about telling them to move out? How do you feel about those same issues now? Do you think they are still very important? (If you don't have children, think about things your parents told you to do or not to do. Did you listen? Why not? How do you feel about those issues now?)

Think about these issues. Then form into small groups to discuss.

If you are a parent discuss this:

Things I told my children, but they didn't listen.

Why they didn't listen. What they said.

How I feel about those issues now.

If you aren't a parent discuss this:

Things my parents told me to do, but I didn't listen.

Why I didn't listen. What I said.

How I feel about these issues now that I am an adult.

What is the most difficult part about being a parent? A child? Explain.

_____

_____

Let's Talk...

1. Parents tell their children to move out for many reasons. Name five.

2. When do children usually move out of their parents' home in your country? Why?

3. When did you move out of your parents' home? Why?

4. What was your family's reaction when you told them you were going to move out?

5. Have you ever regretted moving out of your parents' home? Why or why not?

6. What do you think is the best part of being on your own? What is the worst part of not living at home?

7. Have your parents ever told you or one of your siblings to move out? What did they say? Why did they say that?

8. Do you think it's right for parents to tell their children to move out when they are over eighteen years old? Why or why not? When should adult children move out? Why?

9. Would you ever tell your children to move out? For what reasons, if any? (If you don't have children, imagine what you might do.)

A. Word Search

Try to find your vocabulary words and phrases without looking at the beginning of the lesson. Search across or down. Circle the words and copy them below.

```
d b w v s i b l i n g s r e g r e t a e m
o s i i s s u e e x p l a i p e r b s e o
w c f t c h i l d r e n d u p m h r e e v
n h e d e e t e f a m i v a a a l o a b e
o n y o u r o w n f a v i r r i e t r r o
f l r v e s l y s s h e c p e n u h c o u
a d r e g h u s b a n d e s n u h e h t t
m r r r e t k k b s s u e e t p l r i h i
i a d u l t c h i l d r e n s a c r o s s
l n a t h r e a c t i o n y f a t h e r g
y k t y r l m o t h e r u s i s t e r j l
b d i m m e d i a t e f a m i l y e a d e
```

Can you find any other words? List them. Compare your list with other students.

issue _____ _____ _____ _____

_____ _____ _____ _____ _____

_____ _____ _____ _____ _____

B. Think

Work with a partner. Imagine you are the parents of an adult "child." You want your adult child to move out. Pack a suitcase with ten items you think your child will need. List them in your notebook.

C. Write

If you have moved out of your parents' home, what advice did your parents give you when you decided to move out? What did they tell you? (If you still live at home with your family, what advice do you think they will give you?) Write your answer in your notebook. Discuss this situation with other students.

Lesson 19 Growing Old

Vocabulary New Words

accomplish
achieve
grow (old)
make a
   difference
old
senior citizen
take turns

Let's Talk Words

advantage	golden years	positive light
affect	help	recognized
ail	how old	reflect
cane	leader	refuse
care	lifestyle	retirement
convalescent	mandatory	wheel chair
hospital	media	_____
depict	negative light	_____
distinguished	nursing home	_____
elderly	pass away	_____
fear	plan	_____

Usage

Work with a partner. Choose a picture from the next two pages. Describe the picture using as many vocabulary words as possible. Your partner will draw the picture . Then look at the drawing. Did your partner draw what you described? Now it's your turn to draw. Listen to your partner's description. Take turns describing and drawing.

Let's Start

What do you want people to think and say about you when you become a senior citizen? Answer the following questions. Then share your answers with someone in the class.

1. Where did you grow up?

2. What did you like to do when you were very young?

3. Did you ever help anyone? Who? How did you make a difference in that person's life?

4. How do you treat your family and friends?

5. What have you achieved or accomplished?

6. What kind of person are you?

Let's Talk...

1. What are five fears that you have about growing old?

2. How "old" is old? Why? Explain.

3. What are some advantages people have when they become senior citizens?

4. How can older people help younger people? How can younger people help older people? Give some examples.

5. In the United States, many senior citizens need special care. They live in places called convalescent hospitals or nursing homes. Where do ailing seniors live in your country?

6. Some people become famous, distinguished, or recognized leaders after they enter their "golden years." Name a few of these people. What did they accomplish?

7. Was there an elderly person in your life who was special to you when you were a child? How did that person affect your life?

8. What plans have you made for your retirement? How do you think your lifestyle will change when you become a senior citizen?

9. Do you think there should be mandatory retirement for people over 65? Why or why not?

10. How have people in your county treated senior citizens? Explain.

11. How does the media depict older people? Do TV shows or movies generally show aging in a positive or negative light? Give some examples.

12. What are the "golden years"? Do you think that your older years will be "golden"? Why or why not?

A. Pronunciation

Pronounce these words with your teacher. Then pronounce them with a partner. Do you hear the sound [t], [d], or [id]? Write the final "ed" sound. Then, circle all the words where the "e" in the final "ed" is pronounced. What letters come before the final "ed" so that the "e" is pronounced?

1. baked _____
2. cleaned _____
3. walked _____
4. fixed _____
5. watched _____

6. listened _____
7. planted _____
8. studied _____
9. regretted _____
10. hoped _____

11. visited _____
12. played _____
13. worked _____
14. learned _____
15. decided _____

16. liked _____
17. talked _____
18. loved _____
19. cooked _____
20. passed away _____

Now use these verbs to answer the questions in Exercise **B**.

B. Write

Imagine you are in your golden years. Sit on a park bench and reflect on your life.

1. Do you remember your accomplishments, achievements, failures, adventures, some joyous and some somber events? Share your thoughts.

   _____

   _____

2. Have you had any regrets? How can you change your life and lifestyle now to avoid further unhappiness and failures?

   _____

   _____

C. Draw

In your notebook, draw a picture of your life now. Include your lifestyle, family, friends, employment, and whatever else is important to you. Then, imagine you are ninety-nine years old. Draw a picture of the life you plan to have at that age. Is it a positive or negative picture? What do most people think about growing old? Discuss your pictures and ideas in a group.

My life now   **When I am ninety-nine years old**

Lesson 20 Pollution and Recycling

Vocabulary New Words

aluminum
bottle
can
garbage

glass
noise
pollution
paper
plastic
pollute
pollution
problem
recycle

smog
store
styrofoam
waste

Let's Talk Words

active
concern
conserve
contribute
convince
depend on
director
earth
eliminate

environmental
    group
force
frequent
gasoline
improve
recycling center
resources
safe
volunteer

Usage

Work with a partner. Decide the answers together. Use your vocabulary words and other words you know to write as many possibilities as you can. Share your ideas with the class.

Smog is caused by _____.

Recycled aluminum cans are made into _____.

Recycled paper is used for _____.

Noise pollution is caused by _____.

Recycled styrofoam can be used for _____.

Recycled plastic is used to make _____.

Glass and bottles are recycled at _____.

Garbage and waste can be stored _____.

Let's Start

The president put your group in charge of improving your local city's environment. Make a list of all the environmental problems in your city. Then make a list of how these problems will be corrected.

Present environmental problems	How they will be corrected

Let's Talk...

1. What are five things that can be recycled? Name five things that can't be recycled and explain why.

2. Have you ever recycled anything? What and why? If not, why not?

3. What are some things that are recycled in your country?

4. The United States has government recycling centers. People bring things that can be recycled to the centers, and they receive money for them. Are there recycling centers in your country? If so, how much do people get paid for each item recycled? If not, why do you think there aren't any recycling centers?

5. Do you think people should be forced to recycle? Why or why not?

6. What are five things that cause pollution? What can be done to eliminate pollution?

7. What is carpooling? Why do most people drive alone instead of carpooling? Give three reasons.

8. What environmental groups are active in your country? Have you ever contributed your time as a volunteer to an environmental group? Why or why not?

9. Do you think smaller families usually use fewer resources, or do you believe it depends on the individual family's concern for the environment? Explain.

10. What are landfills? Where are they in your country? Do you think they are safe for the environment? Why or why not?

11. How do you think we can make the earth a cleaner and better place in the future?

A. Survey

Ask students about these environmental issues.

Name	Anna			
Recycle	yes ☑ no ☐	yes ☐ no ☐	yes ☐ no ☐	yes ☐ no ☐
What	newspapers			
Where	at school			
Carpool	yes ☑ no ☐	yes ☐ no ☐	yes ☐ no ☐	yes ☐ no ☐
When	every day			
Where	to school			
With whom	my sister			
Conserve resources	yes ☑ no ☐	yes ☐ no ☐	yes ☐ no ☐	yes ☐ no ☐
What	water, gasoline			

How do students improve the environment? Do most students in your class carpool?
What is the most frequently recycled item?

B. Think

Make a list of everything that can be recycled in your city. Circle the things that you
recycle. Compare your list with other students. Do you recycle the same things?
What else can you recycle?

_____   _____   _____

_____   _____   _____

C. Write

You and a partner are directors of an environmental group. Name your group. What will
your group plan to do to help the environment? How will people be convinced to join
your group? Write your ideas in your notebook. Then share them with the class.

Lesson 21 The Homeless and Welfare

Vocabulary New Words

anyone
find out
homeless
represent
services
social worker
someone
welfare

Let's Talk Words

aid	jobless	specific
assist	low cost	success
business	housing	successful
change (money)	needs	suggest
cross out	offer	support
depressed	poverty	system
food stamps	private	the best way
give reasons	profession	unemployed
hunger	program	unhealthy
in order for	provide	utility rates
individual	public assistance	_____
job counselor	receive	_____

Usage

Work in a small group. Draw some pictures you believe will represent the life of someone who is homeless. Then use your vocabulary words to tell a story about your pictures.

Let's Start

Work in pairs. Read the situation below. Decide who will play the role of the social worker and who will play the role of the homeless person. Role play.

Social worker: How long have you been homeless?

Homeless person: _____.

Social worker: How did you become homeless?

Homeless person: _____.

Social worker: How did you find out about our services?

Homeless person: _____.

How can I find a job? Do you know anyone who would hire me?

Social worker: _____.

Homeless person: Where are some places I can stay until I start working again?

Social worker: _____.

Homeless person: What are some other ways I can change my life?

Social worker: _____.

Let's Talk...

1. Give some reasons why people become homeless.

2. Do you know anyone who was or is homeless? Explain.

3. Have you ever seen any homeless people on the street? What do you do when you see them? Have you ever given a homeless person anything? What? Why?

4. What do you think is the best way to help a homeless person? Give an example.

5. What are some things that individual people in your country do to help poor people?

6. Are there any homeless people in your country? What does the government do to help them?

7. In the United States a welfare system helps to provide assistance to some individuals who cannot support themselves or their families. Food stamps, low-cost housing, shelters, reduced utility rates, and sometimes money are offered by the government. What do you think about this?

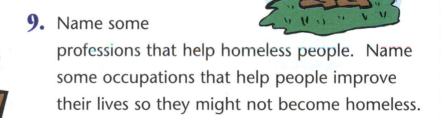

8. Does a public assistance or welfare system exist in your country? Why or why not? If there is one, do you know anyone who is or was receiving assistance? Who? Why did that person need help?

9. Name some professions that help homeless people. Name some occupations that help people improve their lives so they might not become homeless.

10. If you were the president or leader of your country, how would you end poverty?

A. Think

What are some questions that the homeless ask other people? What are some of their needs? (Use the words *some* or *any*.)

Question

*Do you have **any** change?*

_____

_____

_____

_____

Need

*I want to buy **some** coffee.*

_____

_____

_____

_____

B. Choose

Work with a partner. Cross out the word in each row that doesn't belong. Discuss why you crossed out that word.

1. week	poverty	hunger	neediness	welfare
2. homeless	unhealthy	unemployable	successful	depressed
3. give	aid	steal	help	teach
4. food stamps	welfare	salary	public assistance	low-cost housing
5. social worker	teacher	job counselor	doctor	jobless person

C. Write

Work with a partner. Write a letter to the president or leaders of your country encouraging them to end homelessness. Suggest ways private businesses, community volunteers, and the government can contribute to a successful program.

_____

_____

_____

_____

_____

Lesson 22

Vocabulary New Words

	fire	storm
	flood	tornado
	food	volcano
	poisoning	war
	insect	
bomb	infestation	
category	natural	
disaster	disaster	
drought	oil spill	
earthquake	plague	

Let's Talk Words

blow	homeowner	predict
damages	human race	roam
dinosaur	insurance	salesperson
disaster proof	policy	scientist
effect	insure	survival
erupt	lack of	unseasonable
extinct	major	use up
flock	natural	useful
food supply	resource	weather
futuristic	pattern	_____
guarantee	population	_____

Usage

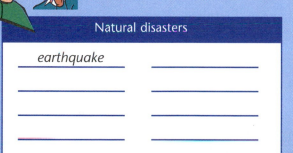

Work with a partner. Read the vocabulary words to each other. Some of the words can be associated with natural or other disasters. Decide in which category you think the words belong. Write them below.

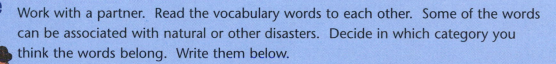

Natural disasters		Other disasters	
earthquake	_____	oil spill	_____
_____	_____	_____	_____
_____	_____	_____	_____
_____	_____	_____	_____

Let's Start

Listen. Raise your hand if the following disasters have ever occurred in your city. Look around the room. How many students have raised their hands? Introduce yourself to these students after class, and ask them about their experiences.

_____ earthquake	_____ tornado	_____ storm
_____ war	_____ food poisoning	_____ bomb
_____ plague	_____ oil spill	_____ fire
_____ volcano	_____ insect infestation	_____ drought

Which disasters are the most common? Do you think that they are the most common throughout the world? Discuss as a class.

Let's Talk...

1. What is a "natural" disaster? Give some examples.

2. Give some examples of other disasters?

3. Why do you think natural disasters occur? Give three reasons. What causes other disasters?

4. What was the most recent natural disaster that happened in your city? Talk about it.

5. Have you ever lived through a major disaster? Where? Who was responsible for it? Why did it happen? How has it affected your life? Talk about it.

6. Has anyone you've known lived through a major disaster? How did it affect that person's life?

7. What do you think was the world's worst disaster? Why do you think it was the worst disaster?

8. What are natural resources? Name at least ten. Tell why some are important or useful.

9. Lack of natural resources can become a major disaster in the future. What can we do to conserve our natural resources?

10. Some people think they can predict a disaster. For example, some people say birds flock together in an unusual pattern. Others say there is unseasonable weather before an earthquake. Do you know any other superstitions or have you heard any other predictions about volcanos erupting or tornados blowing? What are they?

11. Some scientists believe dinosaurs roamed the earth until a major disaster occurred that made them all extinct. What do you think the world will look like five hundred years from now? What disasters will have occurred? What animals will have become extinct? What will have happened to the human race? Use your imagination.

A. Survey

Ask students about their experiences with disasters. Complete the chart.

Name	Native country	Disaster you have experienced	How it affected your life	How will you prepare for a similar disaster?

What disasters have many of the students in your class experienced? Are some disasters common to a particular country?

B. Think

Imagine it is December 1 and you are a homeowner. A salesperson offers you a special end of the year homeowner's insurance policy that guarantees all damages to your home will be insured for the following year. To receive this policy, your home will have to be as disaster proof as possible. What *will you have done* to your home by the end of the year to receive this offer?

1. **earthquake**   *We **will have moved** all mirrors away from our beds.*

2. **flood**   _____ .

3. **fire**   _____ .

4. **tornado**   _____ .

5. **insect infestation**   _____ .

C. Write

Work with a partner. Imagine a futuristic disaster and write about the effects it will have on the environment, population, food supply, and animal survival. Write your ideas in your notebooks. Then share them with the class.

Lesson 23   # Smoking

Vocabulary **New Words**

ban
cigarette
correct
dash
debate
farmer
gallows

hang
hangman
idea
incorrect
industry
non-smoker
smoke
smoker
spell
tobacco

Let's Talk Words

bad habit
bother
break a habit
cancer
chew
could
determine
illegal
instead
permit
quit

second-hand smoke
since
surgeon general
tempt
try
_____
_____
_____
_____
_____
_____

Usage

Form into two teams. Your teacher will choose a word, copy the gallows on the board, and draw dashes next to it. Each dash will represent a letter of the chosen word. Students from each team will take turns guessing letters to spell out the word. Each time a student says an incorrect letter the teacher will draw a body part (beginning with the head) on the gallows. Whoever guesses the word correctly has to use the word in a sentence. If the word isn't used correctly in a sentence, then the other group can try. After a student uses the word correctly in a sentence, that student's group gets a point. The group with the most points wins. (If no group guesses correctly, or if a person is hanging on the gallows, the teacher gets a point. The teacher can win, too.) Close your books and begin.

Hangman

Let's Start

Work in the same groups. One group will represent the tobacco industry farmers and smokers. The other group will represent doctors and non-smokers. Your teacher will make a chart on the board. Debate the following topic: Should cigarettes be banned? Your teacher will write your ideas on the chart. See which side forms the longest list. Then copy your teacher's chart in your notebook.

Cigarettes should be banned	**Cigarettes shouldn't be banned**

Let's Talk...

1. Why do people smoke? Give five reasons.

2. When do people smoke?

3. Do you know people who smoke? Who?
   Does it bother you that they smoke?
   Why or why not?

4. Do you smoke? Why? Why not? If you
   do, how did you feel after your very first cigarette?

5. If you smoke, how long have you been a smoker? Have you ever
   tried to quit, but couldn't? Why don't you quit smoking?

6. If you were a smoker, how long has it been since you quit smoking?
   How do you feel about quitting? How did you stop smoking? Have
   you ever felt tempted to go back to smoking again? Explain.

7. Do you believe that people could get
   cancer from second-hand smoke?
   Why or why not?

8. In many cities in the United States, smoking is banned in supermarkets, restaurants, hospitals, department stores, airplanes, and most forms of public transportation. Do you think that people should be permitted to smoke on airplanes, buses, or trains? Why or why not? Should people be allowed to smoke in public places? Why or why not?

9. Is smoking banned anywhere in your country? Where? Is there a legal age for smoking in your country? If so, what is it? If not, should there be?

10. Do you think that smoking should become illegal? Why or why not?

11. What has the surgeon general determined about smoking? (*What does it say on most cigarette boxes?*)

12. Whose "rights" are more important, smoker's or non-smokers? Why?

A. Survey

Ask students about smoking.

Name	Native country	Who smokes in your family?	Have you ever smoked cigarettes?	How many a day?	Did you quit?

Which country has the most smokers? The fewest smokers?

B. Decide

Smoking is a bad habit that *should* be broken. List some other bad habits. Then decide what *could* be done to break those habits.

Bad habits that *should* be broken	How you *could* break the habit
Smoking is a bad habit that should be broken.	*You could chew gum instead of smoking.*

C. Write

Work with a partner. Talk about the following questions. Then write your ideas. Why should people stop smoking? What might happen if they don't?

People should stop smoking to look better. They could get old-looking skin if they continue to smoke.

_____

_____

_____

Vocabulary

New Words

beat (the odds)
brainstorm
enroll
friendship
gamble
game
job placement

life
location
mean (signify)
pay off
purchase
residence
show
take a chance
win

Let's Talk Words

addiction	force	overwork
alcohol	form	poker
attend	fulfill (dreams)	recovery
beg	Gambler's	revenue
bet	Anonymous	self-help
bingo	hope	group
cheat	horse races	site
crime	lie	slot machine
cycle	lottery	town
excitement	make a bet	_____
famous	overeat	_____

Usage

Where would you see these vocabulary words? Where would you use them? Work with a partner to brainstorm ideas. Write them below.

The sports page of a newspaper   _____

_____   _____

_____   _____

Let's Start

Life is a game or *Life is a gamble* is a popular expression in English. What do you think it means? Have you ever gambled or taken a chance on something important in your life? Did you *beat the odds*? Fill in the chart with important decisions you have made. Then check the box that shows how you feel those decisions paid off. Was it a good decision (you won), or a bad decision (you lost).

Decision or or event	What was the gamble?	Won	Lost	Explain
Telling my friend a secret	*Having gossip spread about me*	☑	☐	*We have a good friendship. She didn't tell.*
		☐	☐	
		☐	☐	
		☐	☐	

Situations people take chances on (gamble on): marriage, children, job placement, enrolling in a class, purchases, location of residence.

Let's Talk...

1. Why do people gamble? Give five reasons.

2. What are five forms of gambling?

3. Do you know anyone who likes to gamble? Who? What games does that person play?

4. Where are five popular places people go to gamble? Where can people play the lottery, bingo, slot machines, or poker? Have you ever played any of those games? Talk about it.

5. When did you gamble last? What game did you play? Where? Did you win or lose the last time you gambled? What did you win or lose?

6. Have you ever beaten the odds at a game and won a lot of money? At what game? Where? When? Do you know anyone else who has? Who?

7. Have you ever gone to a famous gambling town such as Las Vegas, Nevada (United States), or a famous gaming place like Santa Anita horse races in California (United States)? Talk about your experience. What are some famous gambling sites in your country?

8. Have you ever gambled and lost a lot of money? Tell your group about it.

9. Is gambling legal in your country? What kind, if any? If not, why isn't it legal? Do you think that gambling should be legal or illegal? Why?

10. What should the government do about people who spend all their money on gambling? Should they be forced to attend a recovery or *self-help group* such as Gamblers Anonymous? Why or why not?

11. Gambling is an addiction. Other addictions some people have are: alcohol, overeating, oversleeping, and overworking. What addiction(s) do you have? Do you think you could break your addictive cycle? How could you try?

A. Survey

Ask students if they have gambled and find out if they were successful.

Name	Native country	Have you ever made a bet?	Where?	What kind?	Did you win or lose?

What is the most common type of gambling? Do people usually win or lose?

B. Think

Gambling has both positive and negative effects on society. Work with a partner. Look at the words below that are associated with gambling. What other effects does gambling have on society? Add your own ideas. Then complete the charts.

Positive effects on society		Negative effects on society	
jobs created	_____	*poverty*	_____
_____	_____	_____	_____
_____	_____	_____	_____
_____		_____	

poverty	dreams fulfilled	cheating	begging
jobs created	losers	lies	millionaire
revenue	winners	crime	_____
stealing	hope	excitement	_____

C. Write

Chose one question. Talk about it with a partner. Then write a story in your notebook.

1. Have you ever beaten anyone at a game or sport? What game or sport? Who? When? Where?

2. Have you ever won anything? What? When? Where? Why?

Lesson 25 War and the Military

Vocabulary New Words

conflict
current
military
neither
nor

Let's Talk Words

both	educate	justify	Red Cross
close	effective	medal	resolve
relationship	engage in	military	reward
defend	enlist	service	risk
devastate	fight	necessary	serve
dilemma	generation	peacetime	soldier
dishonorable	historian	prison	solve
discharge	honorable	punish	United
disobey	discharge	purple heart	Nations
draft	injure	purpose	voluntary
during	involved in	rebuild	wartime

Usage

Work with a partner. Listen to your teacher read the vocabulary words. Decide which have a positive meaning and which have a negative meaning. (Some have neither a positive nor a negative meaning.) Write the words in the category you think they belong.

Positive	
educate	

Negative	
war	

Let's Start

Discuss as a class. What are some current world problems? What countries are at war? What were you doing when you heard about these situations?

Current world problem	Countries at war or in conflict	What were you doing when you heard about this?

Let's Talk...

1. What are five reasons why countries engage in wars?

2. Who fights in your country's military? (Do both men and women help to defend your country?)

3. Is military service voluntary or mandatory? (Do people enlist on their own, or are they drafted?)

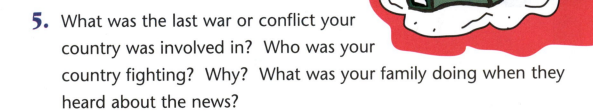

4. Do you think all countries need militaries? Explain.

5. What was the last war or conflict your country was involved in? Who was your country fighting? Why? What was your family doing when they heard about the news?

6. Were you or was anyone close to you serving in the military during the last major war in your country? Talk about it.

7. Have you ever lived in a city during wartime? Explain what it was like.

8. What is the United Nations? What purpose does it serve?

9. Has the United Nations been effective in resolving world dilemmas? Give some examples to justify your answers.

10. Do you think war is necessary? Why or why not?

11. What can each country do to avoid war?

12. In the United States soldiers who risk their lives and are injured receive honorable discharges and medals (purple hearts). Soldiers who disobey orders receive dishonorable discharges, and some go to prison. How are soldiers rewarded and punished in your country?

13. What can soldiers do to help their country during peacetime?

A. Survey

Ask students about a war or conflict their country fought in. Fill in the chart.

Name	Native country	Who was your country fighting?	When ?	Why were they fighting?

Look at your chart. What are some common reasons for wars? What are other ways to solve countries' problems?

B. Think

Work in pairs. Imagine you work for a volunteer organization like the *Red Cross*. What items would you bring to people whose country had been devastated by war and military conflicts? What suggestions would you give them to help rebuild their country?

Items	Suggestions
food	*start a new government*

C. Write

Imagine you are a historian. Write about the last major war that occurred in your country. (Who was your country fighting? Why were they having this conflict?) Your story will be used to educate future generations. Read your story to other students.

_____

_____

_____

_____

Lesson 26   Money Management

Vocabulary   New Words

account
already
apply
at least
bill
broke (poor)

budget
charge
cheer up
context
credit card
due
earn
forever
join
luxury

money
  management
my treat
of course
paycheck
payment
pay off (bills)
penny
tell me about it

Let's Talk Words

accept
basic
bond (savings)
charity
comfortable
compare
cost
debt
invest

major purchase
manage
  (money)
modify (debts)
nest egg
properly
save
stock
unable
wise

Usage

Work in groups of three. Read the dialog and circle your vocabulary words. Try to guess the meanings of the words from the context.

David: Sue, did you get paid today? Will you go shopping with me?

Sue: Sorry, David. I'm not going to be able to buy anything because every penny of my paycheck has already been spent.
Soon, I'm not going to earn enough to pay my monthly bills.

Dan: Tell me about it. I think I'm going to be broke forever.

Sue: At least you will be able to budget for luxury items. I can't! I'm going to be broke after I pay off all my bills, and I'm not going to be able to buy anything until my credit cards are paid off.

David: I have an idea! I'm going to cheer both of you up. Will you join me for ice cream? It's my treat.

Dan: Of course we will!

Let's Start

Discuss this bill as a class. How much *will* Joe owe if the bill isn't paid by the due date? How much is the company *going to* charge him if he's late?

Telephone Bill	
McSnow, Joe	Billing Period 4-1 to 4-30
94859 River Street Apt. 7	Previous charges $189.76
Los Angeles, CA 91604	Payment received on 3-15 $189.76
Account number 0980 -908	Total due on or before May 1 **$247.92**
Current charges **$247.92**	
A late payment charge of 1.5% will apply after May 11.	

Let's Talk...

1. What are five basic monthly bills most people have to pay?

2. Think about last month. What bills did you have to pay?

3. What necessary items do you buy frequently?

4. What are some luxury items that you buy? Name three.

5. When was the last time you had extra money after paying all your monthly bills? What did you do with the money? Why? Have you ever invested money? How? Will you invest money in the future?

6. What are you going to buy in the future? Name at least five things.

7. When are you going to buy those things? Why are you going to buy them?

8. Have you ever saved money for a major purchase? If yes, for what? If not, why not?

9. Have you ever spent too much money and been unable to pay your bills? What happened? Were you in debt?

10. Do you think if you earned more money you would be able to save more, or do you think you would spend more? Why?

11. Do you think most people budget their money wisely? Why or why not?

12. For what things do you think most people save money? Why do you think that?

A. Survey

How are you and the students in your class going to earn a living in five years? Talk to students and fill in the chart below.

Name	What job do you have now?	Do you earn a comfortable living?	Are you going to try to find a new job?	Will you accept a job in a different country?	Why or why not?

What jobs do most students have now? Are most students willing to move? Why?

B. Think

Make a list of all your present bills. Write how much you spend each month for each item. Make another list of items you want to buy. Write the cost next to them. Are you going to have enough money to buy the luxury items you want? Compare your list to another student's. See how you can modify your debts.

Bills and debts every month	$$$$	Luxury items wanted	$$$$

C. Write

You won the lottery! Are you going to manage your money any differently? How? What will you do with your new nest egg? Will you buy more luxury items, invest in stocks and bonds, give more to charity, or take a long vacation? Write your ideas in your notebook. Then share them with the class.

Vocabulary   New Words

prosper
report
right reason
somebody
view

anybody
begin
copy
nobody
order
poem

Let's Talk Words

advertising	deceptive	prestigious
business	demonstrate	pretend
transaction	disappoint	product
car part	exam	replace
cashier	get away with	short-change
catch	get caught	solution
cheating	insurance	subject
claim	mechanic	surgeon
commercial	medical	themselves
customer	owner	yourself

Usage

Work in pairs. Cover your partner's vocabulary words. Dictate some of those words to your partner. Your partner will write them under the correct heading below. When your partner's chart is complete, your partner can dictate other vocabulary words to you. Then check each other's work.

person	place or thing	action	description
_____	_____	_____	_____
_____	_____	_____	_____
_____	_____	_____	_____

Let's Start

Work in a small group. Read the poem and answer the questions.

Cheaters Never Prosper
Does somebody know the answer to this question?
Can I copy anybody's paper?
What!? Nobody is going to let me cheat!?
I don't care. I'll copy someone's paper when that person isn't looking.
Oh, no! Somebody will catch me.
The teacher will report me.
Society will punish me.
Nobody should cheat.

1. What was this person's view on cheating at the beginning of the poem?
2. Did the person cheat? Why or why not?
3. Is that the right reason for not cheating? Why or why not?
4. What is your reason for not cheating?

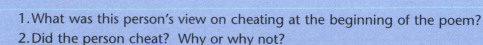

Let's Talk...

1. What are five school subjects many people think are difficult? Which do you think is the most difficult?

2. What are five reasons why people cheat in school? In which subjects do you think people cheat the most? Why?

3. Have you ever cheated in school? Why or why not? If you cheated, did you get away with it, or did you get caught?

4. Have you ever reported anyone who cheated? Why or why not?

5. When you were in school in your country, did you know anyone who cheated on tests? Why do you think that person cheated?

6. If someone were caught cheating in school in your country, what would the teacher do? What do you think the teacher should do?

7. What do you think would happen to society if no one were punished for cheating?

8. What would you do if you found out your friend cheated on a medical exam, and now your friend is going to be a surgeon? Would you tell? Why or why not?

9. Some business owners cheat customers: Some cashiers short-change people, some mechanics replace car parts that don't need to be replaced, and some insurance companies don't pay their claims. Has anyone ever cheated you in a business transaction? Talk about it.

10. Deceptive advertising cheats millions of people a year. Have you ever bought something because you saw someone demonstrate it on a TV commercial and when you tried the product yourself, you were disappointed? Did you feel cheated? What did you do about it?

A. Survey

How do students in your class feel about cheating? Survey them.

Name	Country	Why do you think it is wrong to cheat?	What should happen to someone who cheats?	If you saw someone cheating what would you do?

What do most students think should happen to cheaters? Would most students report someone who cheats?

B. Think

How do people cheat themselves and cheat others? Work with your group to make a list. Then discuss why you think people do these things. Share your ideas with the class.

Cheat themselves
cheat on an exam

Cheat others
sell a used product as new

C. Write

Imagine you're a teacher in a prestigious school. One of your students has cheated on the final exam. In your notebook, write a letter to your student's parents telling them what has happened and what you are going to do about it.

D. Role Play

Now find a student in class. Pretend that student is the parent of the child who cheated. Read your letter to that person, and decide together if your solution to the problem is appropriate.

Lesson 28 Government Spending

Vocabulary   New Words

legal aid	public	space
sanitation	require	exploration
grants	research	mentally ill
disability	ambulance	government
benefits	unemployment	spending
highway	benefits	benefit
dental care	jail	lighting
medical care	repair	
primary	secondary	

street sign
business loan
wildlife
museum

Let's Talk Words

be in charge   tax
collect   wage
donate   _____
government   _____
funding   _____
income   _____
inheritance   _____
power   _____
property   _____

Usage

Many government jobs require employees to be able to alphabetize their records. Practice your skill by alphabetizing your new vocabulary words below.

1. _ambulance_   6. _____   11. _____   16. _____   21. _____
2. _____   7. _____   12. _____   17. _____   22. _____
3. _____   8. _____   13. _____   18. _____   23. _____
4. _____   9. _____   14. _____   19. _____   24. _____
5. _____   10. _____   15. _____   20. _____   25. _____

Let's Start

If your group were in charge of your city's budget of $10,000,000 and each service provided to the public cost $1,000,000, which services would you provide to the people? Circle them. Discuss your choices with the class.

Current services available at $1,000,000 each

free primary school	street repair	hospitals for the mentally ill
free secondary school	free legal aid	child care for the poor
free medical care	food for the poor	medical research
free parks	welfare	student loans and grants
free beaches	sanitation	jails and prisons
space exploration	police	business loans and grants
animal shelters	museums	programs for wildlife
free highways	disability benefits	unemployment benefits
free elderly care	fire department	street signs and lighting
military	libraries	free adult school
ambulance services	homeless shelters	free eye and dental care

Let's Talk...

1. In the United States, the government taxes people on their wages, investment income, most purchases, property, and inheritance. What are five ways other governments collect money?

2. What are five major programs most governments in the world spend money on?

3. What are some programs the government of your country spends money on?

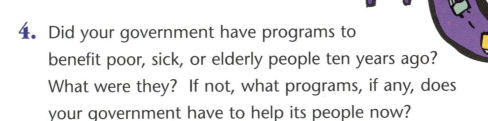

4. Did your government have programs to benefit poor, sick, or elderly people ten years ago? What were they? If not, what programs, if any, does your government have to help its people now?

5. Have you ever received help from any government agency? Why? What government services or programs benefit you? In what way? Explain.

6. Would you be interested in becoming a budget director for your country's government? Why or why not?

7. If you were the president or leader of your country, what would you change in your country's budget?

8. If you could be in charge of all the government's money, what five programs would you put on the top of your list to always receive government funding? Why do you support those programs?

9. If you had the power to cut government spending, what programs would you eliminate? Why?

10. Do you think your government spends its money wisely? Why or why not?

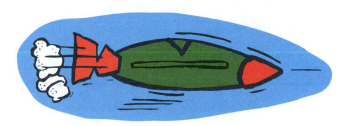

A. Survey

Most governments tax the people. The tax money, or revenue, is used by many governments to provide jobs and services for the people. Make a list of the government jobs and services in your city. Complete the chart and discuss in a group.

Government job or service	Continue or Eliminate		Why?
Public education	☑	☐	An educated public makes a strong society. An uneducated society has more crime.
	☐	☐	
	☐	☐	
	☐	☐	
	☐	☐	
	☐	☐	

B. Decide

Finish these sentences.

If I had to eliminate one government program, I would_____.

If I could create a new government service, I would _____.

If I became the director of the government program, I would _____.

If I had a million dollars to donate, I would_____.

C. Write

Do you think that your city's government budgets its money well? If so, why? If not, how could it budget its money better? Write your answer in your notebook. Discuss your idea with a partner.

Lesson 29 Prejudice and Discrimination

Vocabulary   New Words

against	label
aloud	nationality
assign	prejudice
categorize	raise children
define	separate
different	size
discriminate	social status
discrimination	stereotype
divide	
free (of)	

Let's Talk Words

as well as	law
called (named)	opinion
civil right	personal liberties
Constitution	prevent
document	protect
entitle to	World's Rights
experience	Organization
expose	_____
highest	_____
invite	_____

Usage

Work in a small group. Choose a leader for your group. Your teacher will assign a few of the vocabulary words to each group. Each group will write definitions and defining sentences for the words. When a word is called out by the teacher, the leader of the group who has that word will say the definition and sentence aloud. See if you can understand your new words from the examples given by the groups.

Let's Start

What are some categories that describe people? (How are people frequently separated and divided?) In a group, complete the chart and discuss why you think people are often labeled and stereotyped. Add another category.

Gender	Social Status	Race	Size	Nationality	
Male					
Female					

How do you categorize yourself? How does your group categorize you?

How do people use categories to discriminate against each other? In your native country did people use categories to discriminate? What had happened to cause this type of discrimination?

Describe a world without prejudice or discrimination. How can people raise their children so the next generation will be free of this problem?

Let's Talk...

1. What is prejudice? What is discrimination? Why do you think prejudice and discrimination exist?

2. Do you think there is prejudice or discrimination where you live now? Give an example to support your answer.

3. Was there prejudice or discrimination in your native country? Explain.

4. Have you ever experienced prejudice or discrimination? With whom? Had you done anything to make that person angry? Explain. (If you have never experienced prejudice or discrimination, why do you think you have never been exposed to it?)

5. Before the 1960s, had people done anything to try to eliminate discrimination in your native country? What about after the 1960s?

6. Do you think government programs such as T*he World's Rights Organization* or the *United Nations* have reduced prejudice and discrimination in the world? Why or why not?

7. In the United States people are entitled to certain civil rights and personal liberties. These rights have been guaranteed to them by the Constitution, a document stating the highest law in the country. Are the civil rights of people in your country guaranteed and protected? Why or why not? If they are, how?

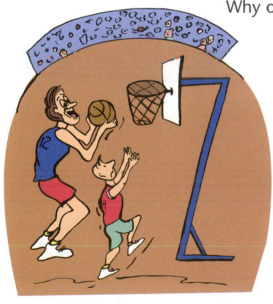

8. How can people change the world in order to eliminate prejudice and discrimination?

9. Is discrimination ever necessary? Do you think it is right to tell a short man that he cannot play basketball? What if he plays as well as the tall players? (Think of other similar examples.)

A. Survey

Find out about other students' experiences with prejudice and discrimination. Complete the chart.

Name	Experience with prejudice or discrimination When? Where? With whom?	What had been your opinion about people before that experience?	What is your opinion now? How has it changed?

Have most people in the class experienced prejudice or discrimination? Are their views different from yours or the same?

B. Think

Work with a partner. What are ways to prevent people from becoming prejudiced? How can we stop them from discriminating against others? How can we change their views if they are already prejudiced, and if they discriminate against others? Write your answers. Share them with the class.

Preventing prejudice and discrimination
Teach young children about people of other races, religions, or cultures.

Changing views
Introduce them to people of other races, religions, or cultures.

C. Write

Do you think it's possible to eliminate prejudice and discrimination? Why or why not? Write your answer in your notebook, and share your thoughts with a student in the class.

Lesson 30

Divorce

Vocabulary New Words

acquire
asset
aware
divorce
faithful
finish
get divorced
identity
react

save
(a marriage)
thoughts
tool
trust
wish

Let's Talk Words

agreement
alimony
be around
child support
ex-spouse
ex-wife
funny
intelligent
joint custody
kind

laugh
lively
marital status
patient
remain
rich
split
wonder
_____
_____

Usage

Mike and Ann would have been married twenty years today. If Mike had ever thought they would have been divorced, he would have done more to save the marriage. He knew there were problems, but he wished he had been more aware of Ann's needs. Finish Mike's thoughts. Work in a small group. Review the vocabulary words and discuss Mike's feelings.

I wish I had been faithful to Ann.   *If I had been faithful, she would have trusted me.*

I wish I had said_____ .   If I _____ .

I wish I had invited _____ .   If I _____ .

I wish I had known _____ .   If I _____ .

I wish I had told Ann _____ .   If I _____ .

I wish I hadn't reacted _____ .   If I _____ .

I wish I hadn't allowed _____ .   If I _____ .

Let's Start

As you know, Mike and Ann have divorced. Invent identities for them. Then look at what was divided between them. If a judge had divided up their assets who do you think would have gotten what?

Joint children and possessions	To Ann	To Mike
a 13-year-old son		
an infant son		
a 4-year-old daughter		
a house		
tools		
pets		

Let's Talk...

1. Why do some people get divorced? Name a few reasons.

2. Are any of your friends or family members divorced? How do you feel about it? How did you react when you heard the news?

3. Have you ever known anyone who was in a bad marriage but would never get divorced? Tell your group about that situation.

4. Have you ever wished someone you've known hadn't gotten a divorce? Who? Why?

5. After a divorce, do you think people should remain friends with their ex-spouse's friends and family? Why or why not?

6. In The United States, it is common for people to separate before a divorce. Why do you think they do that? Do people separate before they divorce in your country?

7. After a divorce, children usually live with their mother. However, in joint custody agreements they split their time between their parents' homes. The father is usually required to pay alimony and child support to his ex-wife. How do you feel about joint custody? What do you think about alimony? Child support? Explain your opinions.

8. You're having a party. Your closest friends have just gotten divorced. You'd like to invite both of them, but they're not talking to each other. Who do you invite? Why? Who do you think will attend?

A. Survey

What is the marital status of the people in your class? Ask them. Complete the chart.

Name	Marital status	How long?	Do you wish your marital status were different?	Why?

Are most people in your class married or single? Who has been married the longest?
Are most happy with their marital status?

B. Think

Lisa has been married to Bob for three years. Now they are divorcing. Lisa, like many
women in this situation, feels she married her husband for the wrong reasons. She
wonders how different her life would have been if she had married any one of her other
boyfriends, instead of Bob. Complete her thoughts by finishing the sentences below.

John was funny. If I had married John, I <u>would have laughed a lot more.</u>

1. Joe was rich. If I had married Joe, I _____ .

2. Bill was intelligent. If I had married Bill, I _____ .

3. Tom was kind. If I had married Tom, I _____ .

4. Greg was patient. If I had married Greg, I _____ .

5. Steve was lively. If I had married Steve, I _____ .

6. Gary was generous. If I had married Gary, I _____ .

7. Mark was fun. If I had married Mark, I _____ .

C. Write

What three things in your life do you wish you had done differently? Write them in your
notebook. Share them with someone in your class.

Calling In Sick

Vocabulary New Words

absent	plumber
artist	secretary
average	sick
call in sick	various
carpenter	writer
housekeeper	
lunch break	
painter	
personnel	

Let's Talk Words

manager
per
previous
sick day
valid

_____
_____
_____
_____

Usage

Work with a partner. Guess which vocabulary word or words best describes what the person is saying. With the remaining words, write your own clues, and have your partner guess the words.

1. "At work, I eat from 12:00 to 12:30."

2. "I'm not well today. I need to tell my boss I won't be able to go to work."

3. "I'm not the best worker, but I'm not the worst. I'm like everyone else."

4. "I'm so happy. It's Wednesday! I never work on Wednesdays."

Let's Start

When people are out sick from work, many work projects aren't done. Work together in a small group as a personnel team. Review a list of all employees who were absent from various companies the day before. Write what wasn't done because those people weren't at work.

What wasn't done	Person who was absent	
The letters weren't typed	by the	secretary .
	by the	plumber .
	by the	teacher .
	by the	cook .
	by the	carpenter .
	by the	painter .
	by the	housekeeper .
	by the	writer .
	by the	artist .

What wasn't done at work or at home because you were sick? Discuss.

Let's Talk...

1. What are five reasons why people call in sick?

2. What is not a good reason to be absent from work?

3. When did you call in sick last? Why?

4. Have you ever called in sick when you weren't sick? Why?

5. Do you believe it's okay to use a sick day when you aren't sick? Why or why not?

6. Do you get paid for sick days at your current job? Why or why not? How about your previous jobs?

7. Do people get paid for sick days in your country? For what jobs?

8. How many paid sick days do you think a person should be allowed to have per year? Why?

9. If you want a day off, do you think it's better to ask for the day off or use a sick day? Why?

10. Imagine you are the manager of a company. An employee has called in sick. Later, after work, you see that employee at a local baseball game. Do you approach him at the game or wait until the next day to talk to him? What will you say?

A. Survey

Fill in the chart. (If the student doesn't work, ask about a previous job or about school.)

Name	Where do you work?	Do you get paid? for sick days?	How often do you call in sick?	When did you call in sick last?	For what reason?

B. Think

Employers are given many reasons by employees to justify why they can't come to work. What are some reasons? After you write your reasons below, work with a partner and circle the items you both think are valid. Then discuss as a class.

_____   _____

_____   _____

_____   _____

C. Decide

Work in a small group. Imagine you own your own company. The people in your group are your employees. Tell them three reasons why they won't be paid for sick days. Write your reasons and their reactions below.

Reason	Reaction

D. Write

Do you think people should be paid for sick days? Write your thoughts in your notebook. Share your ideas with a partner.

Lesson 32

Justice Systems

Vocabulary New Words

court case
fair
forget

guilty
innocent
justice
justice served
justice system
outcome
phrase
should have
verdict

Let's Talk Words

arrest	fit (equal)	prisoner
capital punishment	hindsight	rape
	inmate	right to
commit	legal system	security
corporal punishment	look back	send to prison
	maximum	sentence (court)
crime of passion	minimum	theft
death row	minor	try in court
deserve	mistake	_____
enforce	murder	_____
fist fight	perspective	_____

Usage

Play hangman with your teacher using your vocabulary words. This time the game is more difficult. Your teacher can choose a single word or a phrase. Your teacher will make dashes on the board with spaces between the words to help you out. (If you forgot how to play, see page **89**.)

Hangman

Let's Start

Is there or has there been a court case that has affected you personally or has been of special interest to you? Was the outcome fair? If not, what do you think the verdict should have been? Discuss it with the class.

Court Case	
When/Where?	
Who was involved?	
What happened?	
What was the verdict?	☐ guilty ☐ innocent
Was justice served?	☐ yes ☐ no
If not, what should have been the verdict? Why?	

Let's Talk...

1. What does the word "justice" mean to you? Do you think there is justice in any legal system? Why or why not?

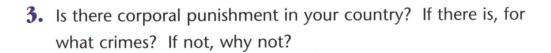

2. What is corporal punishment? What do you think about it? Should it be used in schools? In prisons? Not at all? Why? Explain.

3. Is there corporal punishment in your country? If there is, for what crimes? If not, why not?

4. What is capital punishment? What do you think about it? Do you think a government has a right to enforce capital punishment? If so, for what crimes? If not, why not?

5. Is there capital punishment in your country? If there is, for what crimes? How are death row inmates treated?

6. What are five reasons why people are put in prison in your country?

7. Did you ever know or hear about anyone who was in prison? Was that person guilty of the crime? Should that person have been sent to prison? Why or why not?

8. There are many different kinds of crime: murder, theft, crimes of passion, rape. Which of these do you think deserves the punishment of life in prison? Which of the criminals who commit these crimes do you think should be put in maximum security prisons? Minimum security prisons? Why?

9. Do you think minors should be tried in a court and sentenced as adults? Why or why not?

10. In the United States it's very expensive to keep a person in prison. How do you feel about so much money being spent on prisons and prisoners? Is it the same in your country? Explain.

A. Think

There is crime in every country. List a few crimes that were committed in your country and the punishments that were given for them. Do you think the punishments fit the crimes? If not, write the punishment that you think should have been given. Compare and discuss your list with a few friends in class.

Crime	Punishment given	Punishment you think should have been given	Why?

B. Reflect

Everyone makes mistakes. Hindsight gives you a different perspective on them. Sometimes people look back and think about what they should have done to have had a better outcome. Think about some of the mistakes that you have made in your life. Write them. Next to them write what you should have done. Discuss with a partner.

What happened	What you should have done
I was arrested for being in a fist fight.	*I should have discussed the problem instead of fighting.*

C. Write

Do you think any justice systems are fair? If so, which ones, and why? If not, why not? Write your answer. Use examples to justify your answer. Share your answer with a partner.

Vocabulary   New Words

aspirin
caffeine
classification
cocaine
drug

headache
marijuana
medicine
patient
penicillin
prescription
side effect

Let's Talk Words

ailment	herb	sore throat
backache	ill	stomachache
catch selling	legalize	stuffy nose
catch using	on the street	vomit
constipation	over the	_____
diarrhea	counter	_____
garlic	prescribe	_____
generic	rehabilitation	_____
ginger root	center	_____
ginseng	remedy	_____

Usage

Work with a partner and take turns politely asking each other what the vocabulary words mean. Look at the examples. (If you need help, ask the class, "Who could tell us what _____ means?")

Student A: Do you think you could give me an example of the word *drug*?

Student B: Of course. Alcohol is a *drug*.

Student A: Do you know what *medicine* means?

Student B: Sure. *Medicine* is what doctors give sick patients.

Student A: Would you please tell me what *side effect* means ?

Student B: I'd be happy to. *136 effect* is a negative reaction to a drug. A headache can be an example of a *side effect*.

Let's Start Fill in the chart. Then discuss your answers as a class.

Name	Medicine or drug	Legal or illegal	Do you need a prescription?	What do you think about its classification?
aspirin	*medicine*	*legal*	*no*	*It's correct. Aspirin is useful and has few side effects.*
cocaine				
caffeine				
marijuana				
penicillin				

Add medicines from your own cabinet at home.

Let's Talk...

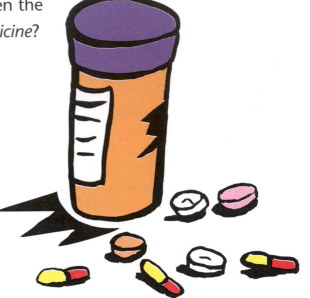

1. What is the difference between the word *drug* and the word *medicine*?

2. What is a generic drug?

3. Why do you think that some medicines are legal while others are illegal?

4. What are five common medicines, prescribed by doctors, that would be illegal if they were bought on the street?

5. What are five popular drugs sold on the streets that doctors are not permitted to prescribe?

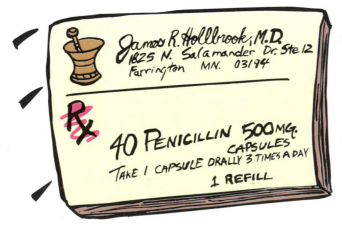

6. What are five reasons people take illegal drugs?

7. What are some common illegal drugs in your country?

8. What happens to people in your country who are caught using illegal drugs? Do they get put in a hospital, in a rehabilitation center, or in jail? Explain.

9. Do you have a friend who has tried an illegal drug? What was that person's experience?

10. When people in your country are ill, do they use herbs such as ginseng, garlic, or ginger root? If so, could you explain how they work? If not, do you know why herbs aren't used?

11. Do you think alcohol is a drug? Why or why not?

12. What do you think would happen if all drugs were legalized? Do you think all drugs should become legalized? Why or why not?

13. Do you have any views about what should happen to a person who's caught using or selling illegal drugs? What are your views?

A. Survey

What do students in your class do when they don't feel well? Find out the natural remedies that students in your class use. Then write down the common medicine prescribed for the ailment.

Ailment	Student's name	Natural remedy	Medicine or doctor's advice
headache			
stomachache			
sore throat			
backache			
stuffy nose			
vomiting			
constipation			
diarrhea			

What are some common home remedies? What do students' doctors recommend for the same illnesses?

B. Think

List the names of some over-the-counter medicines commonly prescribed in your country. (Look in your dictionary to find the English word.) Then, as a class, talk about what those medicines are prescribed for. Discuss any side effects that are believed to be caused by those medications.

Medicine	What it is prescribed for	Common side effects

C. Write

Write about the strongest drug that you have ever needed. Why did you use it? What was your experience? Discuss your answer with a partner.

Lesson 34 What Would You Do If...

Vocabulary

New Words

conclusion
creative
develop
fluently
logical
paragraph
pound
swell up
translator
weigh

Let's Talk Words

admit
bookkeeper
born
discover
embezzle
fail
final
fond of
grant
human being
kill

magic lamp
notify
overhear
read minds
turn around
_____
_____
_____
_____
_____

Usage

Work with a partner. Match the first part of the sentence with the logical conclusion.

1. If I weighed 300 pounds,
2. If I spoke five languages fluently,
3. If I had had enough money,
4. If I were a teacher,
5. If I had a job,
6. If I had bought the correct shoe size,
7. If I hadn't eaten the old food,
8. If I had arrived late to work again,

a. I would have been fired.
b. I would be very patient.
c. I would be a translator.
d. I wouldn't have gotten sick.
e. I would have bought the car.
f. I would need a diet.
g. My feet wouldn't have swelled up.
h. I would buy a new computer.

Let's Start

Look at the *Usage* section above. Choose the beginning of one of the numbered sentences and write an ending for it. Then, using as many vocabulary words as possible, write a short paragraph to develop your idea. Share it with someone in class.

_____

_____

_____

After you finish, write new endings to the rest of the sentences in your notebook. Work with a partner. Be creative!

Let's Talk...

1. If you won $1,000,000, what would you buy? Name at least three things.

2. If you were allowed to be the leader of any country in the world, which country would you choose? Why? What changes would you make in that country?

3. If you had three wishes, what would you wish for? Why? (You can't wish for money or more wishes.)

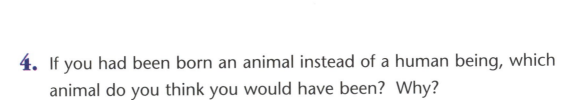

4. If you had been born an animal instead of a human being, which animal do you think you would have been? Why?

5. During lunch in a local restaurant, you overhear someone admit to killing another person. You turn around to see who it is, and you know that person. Would you notify the police? Why or why not?

6. If you were a teacher and one of your friends who enrolled in your class didn't pass the final exam, would you fail your friend? Why or why not?

7. If you were a doctor and you became very fond of one of your patients, could you call that patient and ask for a date? Why or why not?

8. If you worked in a big company and discovered the bookkeeper was embezzling money, would you tell your supervisor? What if you knew the bookkeeper had a sick child at home and had a lot of medical bills? What if the bookkeeper were your friend?

9. Have you ever wished you were born in another place or time? Where and when did you wish you had been born? Why?

A. Decide

Complete these sentences. Discuss your answers in a group.

If I had been born in 1850, I _____ .

If I had gotten the job I wanted, I _____ .

If I were five years old again, I_____ .

If I could read people's minds, I _____ .

If I had traveled more, I _____ .

B. Think

You find a magic lamp. Now you have six wishes: three to change things you regret in your past and three to change your future. What do you wish?

I wish I had . . .	I wish I . . .
_____	_____
_____	_____
_____	_____

Now look for students who wish for the same things. Write the names of the students who have at least one of the same wishes as you. Talk with them about their choices.

_____ _____ _____

_____ _____ _____

_____ _____

C. Write

Imagine you had the power to make three people's wishes come true. Who would you grant wishes to? Why? What do you think they would wish for? Write your answer. Then discuss it with someone in the class.

_____

_____

_____

Lesson 35   Employment Issues

Vocabulary   New Words

career	section
classified	telecommute
could have	vacation
flexibility	
in house	
job security	
pension plan	
priority	

Let's Talk Words

available	occasional
boss	performance
confront	promote
damage	reputation
directions	_____
following	_____
incentive	_____
might have	_____

Usage

You might get the opportunity to look for a (new) job. Work in pairs. Look in the classified section of a local newspaper or magazine. Circle as many of your new vocabulary words as you can. Try to understand their meanings from the context. Could you have found these words in another source? Where? (If there are no newspapers or magazines in your classroom, circle the *Let's Talk* vocabulary words on the next two pages, and guess their meanings from the context.)

Let's Start

What is most important to you in a career choice? Number the following items from 1 to 10. (1 is the highest priority, 10 the lowest). Then discuss your choices in a small group.

_____ salary	_____ job security
_____ medical benefits	_____ retirement/pension plan
_____ schedule flexibility	_____ in house child care
_____ vacation pay	_____ telecommute days
_____ sick pay	_____ disability benefits

Let's Talk...

1. What are some incentives your current job offers? If you aren't employed at this time, talk about incentives you had at a previous job.

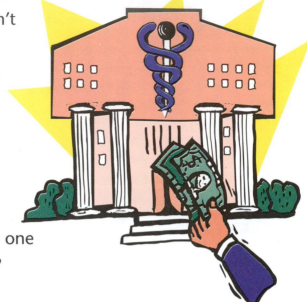

2. What do you think you should do if you have more than one supervisor and each one gives you different directions?

3. What are some things you can do if you don't get along with someone at work? Was there someone at a past job you didn't get along with? What could you have done differently to get along with that person better?

4. Imagine you and your friend work at the same company. You know you work harder and do a better job than your friend. To your surprise, your friend gets a promotion and is now *your* supervisor. What do you do?

5. Imagine your supervisor is making poor decisions for the company. Do you say anything? Why or why not?

6. What would you do if you heard office gossip that could damage a co-worker's reputation? Would you confront the people who spread the gossip, tell your co-worker, or do nothing? Why?

7. Think about this situation: You have a boss who asks you to go out to lunch. You refuse, but the following day, your boss asks you out again. You feel very uncomfortable about this. What can you do? If this had happened to you at a previous job, what do you think you might have done?

8. If the same salary and benefits were offered by all available employers for all jobs, which job would you choose? Why?

9. If you had known when you were younger what you now know about jobs and careers, what might you have done differently to be better prepared for the career you want?

A. Survey

Everyone has an occasional bad day at work. Ask students about problems they have had at work and how they were resolved.

Name	Country	Problem you had at work	How it was resolved

What are some common job problems? How are they usually dealt with? What would the ideal work situation be for you?

B. Role Play

What do you say when your supervisor gives you a negative review and you feel you don't deserve it? If you were the supervisor how would you respond?

Work in pairs to role play. One student will play the part of the supervisor and the other the employee. The supervisor talks to the employee about poor work performance. The employee feels the work has been above average.

C. Write

Look at question number **5** in the *Let's Talk* section. What do you think might have happened if you told your boss he or she was making poor decisions? Why? (If you aren't working now, think about a previous supervisor.) Write your answer below. Share it with the class.

_____

_____

_____

_____

Vocabulary **New Words**

amusement park	light
attendant	must
cancel	really
estimate	safety
even though	smell
excuse	taste
extremely	terrible
funeral	twice
heavy	
lady	

Let's Talk Words

catch in a lie
difference
make up
request
think back
white lie

_____
_____
_____
_____

Usage

Work in a group. Decide if the people in these situations are telling lies or making up excuses. Try to understand your vocabulary words from the context.

John must cancel plans with his cousin to finish his work. He's already canceled plans with him twice this month. Both times John told his cousin that he must work. He feels he can't tell him the same thing again, even though it's the truth. So, this time he tells him he's sick.

An amusement park attendant asks a heavy lady to estimate how much she weighs. He says he must know for safety reasons. The woman is embarrassed. She tells the attendant she's fifty pounds lighter than she really is.

Kathy's at a friend's house for dinner. The food smells extremely bad, and has a terrible taste. When her friend tells her to eat some more, Kathy says that the food was really good, but she must stay on her diet. (Kathy isn't on a diet.)

Let's Start

What are some excuses people give when they refuse a date? Which of these are usually true and which are usually lies?

Excuses	Usually true	Usually a lie
I have to wash my hair.	☐	☑
I'm going to a funeral.	☑	☐
	☐	☐
	☐	☐
	☐	☐

Let's Talk...

1. What is the difference between a lie and an excuse?

2. What are five common excuses people use when they don't want to do something?

3. What are three lies or excuses that you frequently hear?

4. Who lied to you last? When? How did you feel when you found out the truth?

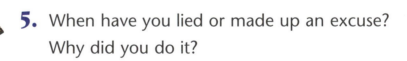

5. When have you lied or made up an excuse? Why did you do it?

6. Have you ever confronted someone who lied to you? Why or why not?

7. Have you ever told a "white lie"? How is this different from any other lie (or excuse)?

8. Have you ever been caught in a lie? When? What did you say?

9. Why do you think some people frequently lie or make up excuses instead of telling the truth?

10. In a popular children's story about a boy named Pinocchio, Pinocchio's nose grows every time he tells a lie. His nose becomes very big because he lies so much. Is there a children's story in your country that teaches children not to lie? Tell the story.

11. Imagine a world where everyone must always tell the truth. Describe this world. Do you think that in some situations it is better to lie or make up an excuse? Why or why not?

A. Reflect

Think back to when you were a child. Try to remember the things that your parents told you you must and mustn't do. What problems did you have when you didn't listen? What did you tell them when things went wrong? Did you tell the truth, or did you make up a lie or an excuse? Complete the chart. Then share your answers with a few students.

My parents told me I must or I mustn't	What went wrong	What I told them
My parents told me I must study.	*I didn't study and I didn't pass the test.*	*Everyone failed because the test was very difficult.*

B. Think

Many professionals tell people what they must or mustn't do. What have professionals told you to do? When they ask you if you have done what they requested, and you haven't, what do you tell them? Share your answers with someone in the class.

My doctor told me I must _____ .

My doctor told me I mustn't _____ .

The reason I gave why I didn't do what my doctor suggested was _____ .

My teacher told me I must _____ .

My teacher told me I mustn't _____ .

The reason I gave why I didn't do what my teacher suggested was _____ .

C. Write

Did you ever feel you must make up an excuse or lie? Why? Write about that time. (If not, how do you think you have avoided these kinds of situations?)

Lesson 37   Forms of Government

Vocabulary

New Words

capitalism
communism
form of government
information
prime minister
ruler
socialism
world leader

Let's Talk Words

decision	_____
global economy	_____
mention	_____
operate	_____
stand for	_____
_____	_____
_____	_____

Usage

Form into small groups. Name some people or countries that can or could have been associated with these vocabulary words.

1. capitalism _____   _____
2. communism _____   _____
3. socialism _____   _____
4. world leader _____   _____
5. prime minister _____   _____
6. ruler _____   _____

Let's Start

Discuss the following questions as a class. (Complete the chart with the information you hear in class.) Name some important government and world leaders. Are any of them in power now? How long have these leaders been in power? How have they changed their country? How have their changes affected the world?

Leader's name	Country	How has that leader changed his or her country?	How have those changes affected the world?

Let's Talk...

1. What are some common forms of government? Name at least three.

2. What form of government did your native country have five years ago? Explain. Does your country have the same form of government today? Why or why not?

3. Who was the leader, president, prime minister, or ruler of your native country five years ago? Was that person a good leader? Why or why not? Who's the leader of your country today?

4. Who are some other important leaders in your country? What issues do they stand for? Do you approve of their leadership? Why or why not?

5. What is a global economy? How has it changed or how is it changing the form of government in your country?

6. What positive or negative decisions has the president of the country you are living in now made recently? Were they major decisions? Have they affected your life?

7. What governmental changes have there been in your country recently?

8. Who do you think has been a great world leader? Why?

9. What kind of government do you think is best for most people? Why?

10. If you were the leader of the country that you're now living in, what three things would you change first? Why?

A. Survey

What do the students in your class think about the government in their native countries? What is good about it, and what needs to be changed? Fill out the chart below.

Name	Native country	Form of government	Leader	Positive about system	Changes needed

What are the most common forms of government? What is positive about government rule? What were the changes most frequently mentioned?

B. Think

With a partner, discuss what you like and dislike about the following three forms of government. Write your views below.

Type of government	Like	Dislike
Communism		
Socialism		
Capitalism		

C. Write

In a group, invent a new form of government to rule your country. Discuss how it will operate. Will there be leaders? If so, who? What will be their roles? If not, why not? How are the people in the country involved? Write your ideas below.

_____

_____

Lesson 38   Professionalism

Vocabulary   New Words

	librarian	renewal
	marketing	review (at work)
	manager	TV series
	meeting	TV show ratings
	must have	
appearance	past life	
character actress	personality	
comedian	politician	
contract	profession	
hair stylist	professionalism	
lawyer	psychic	

Let's Talk Words

accountant	true
background	professional
break down	trustworthy
dishonest	unethical
earn a living	unprofessional
employ	unskilled
ethical	workforce
influence	_____
pursue	_____
take	_____
advantage of	_____

Usage

Imagine you and your partner are psychics. You help people find careers by looking up their professions in a past life. Study the students in your class. Which students do you think must have had these professions in a past life? (Use their appearances and personalities to make your decisions.) Write the student's name next to the profession. How are people and jobs stereotyped?

hair stylist _____   artist _____   actor/actress _____

doctor _____   lawyer _____   comedian _____

teacher _____   salesperson _____   secretary _____

police officer _____   librarian _____   politician _____

Let's Start

Form into small groups. In your group decide what must have happened to these people.

1. When Bob came home from work he was very depressed. He told his family he needed to find another job. What must have happened?

2. Peggy had her yearly review yesterday. She left the meeting smiling. Today she drove to work in a new car. What must have happened?

3. Lisa has been upset all day. She has worked hard for three years as a character actress in a TV series. Her contract is up for renewal this week. Marketing managers have told her the TV show's ratings have been low. What must have happened?

Now talk to the class about your professional life.

Let's Talk...

1. What are five professions that have a reputation for employing trustworthy and honest people?

2. What professions have a reputation for employing unprofessional, unethical, and unskilled individuals?

3. What job did you have in your country? Did you like it? Why or why not?

4. What is your profession now? How do most people view what you do for a living?

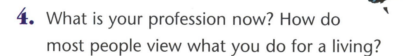

5. What is the difference between a job and a career? What jobs or careers did your parents have? How did you feel about what they did to earn a living? Why?

6. When you were a child, what career did you think you would pursue when you grew up? Do you have that job now? Are you currently trying to get that job? Why or why not?

7. Have you ever met a dishonest professional? Have you ever been taken advantage of in a business transaction? Talk about your experience.

8. What is a "true professional"? Talk about a professional person who helped improve your life.

9. Before the 1960s most women in the United States didn't work outside their homes. What must have happened to make women decide to change their lifestyle and go into the workforce?

A. Survey

Ask students about the professions they hope to have someday, what their duties will be, and who must have influenced their career decisions the most?

Name	Job	Duties	Who must have influenced your career decisions most?	Why?

Who must have had the biggest influence on most students' job choice? A family member? A teacher? Someone else?

B. Think

Most professionals are ethical, but unfortunately some aren't. Work with a partner and discuss how these dishonest professionals could take advantage of the people they are supposed to be helping. What should the people do if they have been taken advantage of? Fill in the chart below. Then discuss your answers.

Profession	What could happen if the person is unethical?	Who should the unethical behavior be reported to ?
Used car salesperson	*The salesperson sells you a car that breaks down.*	*Report that person to the sales manager.*
Lawyer		
Doctor		
Accountant		

C. Write

Think about question **8** in the *Let's Talk* section. Write about a professional who has helped you improve your life. Give some background information on this individual and describe how this person has helped you. Explain why you think this person is an outstanding professional.

Lesson 39   Success

Vocabulary New Words

close friend
decent
integrity
keep
own
possess
possession
powerful
rare
valuable

Let's Talk Words

achievement   personal contact
anniversary   renowned
business contact   social life
generally   type of
goal   work hard
in mind   _____
in terms of   _____
keep in touch   _____
network   _____
organize   _____

Usage

Another *word association* game. Your teacher will choose a vocabulary word. What word can be associated with that word? Shout out a word on this page, or any vocabulary word from a previous lesson. Your teacher will write all the words on the board. See how successful you have been at acquiring your vocabulary.

Teacher: *own*
Students: *possess, have, keep*

Let's Start

Success has different meanings to different people. How do you define success? Number the following from 1 to 10. (1 is the highest priority, 10 the lowest) Then form into small groups and discuss your choices.

_____ being in a happy marriage

_____ having a fulfilling career

_____ keeping many close friends

_____ possessing a lot of money

_____ being faithful to a religion

_____ having a decent family with good children

_____ owning many rare and valuable possessions

_____ being very powerful

_____ having integrity and doing what is right

_____ being very famous

Let's Talk...

1. What is success? What are five ways a person can be successful?

2. Have you achieved any goals you have made for yourself? If so, which ones? If not, why not?

3. In the United States, many people think of success in terms of money and fame. With this definition in mind, who do you consider to be successful? Where do they live? What have they accomplished?

4. How is success generally defined in your country? Name a world renowned successful person from your country. Why is that person so successful? What do you think that person must have done to become so successful?

5. Have you had success in this English class? What could you have done to be more successful?

6. Who would you say is successful in your family? Why?

7. Do you believe people must work hard to become successful? Why or why not?

8. Is being successful important to you? Why or why not?

9. Do you have the kind of success you want in your life? If so, what have you done to become successful? If not, what do you think you should have done? What can you do now?

10. What type of success do you think you might have in the future? How will you prepare for it?

A. Network

In order to have a successful career or social life one should network by keeping in touch with friends. It is also important to make business and personal contacts often. Ask two students in your class the following information so you can keep in touch with them.

Name _____ Phone number __(___)_____

Address_____

City _____ State / Country _____ Zip Code _____

Occupation _____ Hobbies _____

Spouse's name _____ Spouse's occupation _____ Anniversary _____

Children's names and ages_____

Name _____ Phone number __(___)_____

Address_____

City _____ State / Country _____ Zip Code _____

Occupation _____ Hobbies _____

Spouse's name _____ Spouse's occupation _____ Anniversary _____

Children's names and ages_____

B. Role Play

Work with a partner. Think about question **10** in the *Let's Talk* section. You have an idea you hope will be successful. Imagine your partner will be the person who helps you achieve that goal. Who would your partner be? How would you ask for the help you need? What would you say? Organize your thoughts. Then role play.

My goal is to_____ .

My partner would be _____ .

I would say _____ .

C. Write

Who is the most successful person you know? In your notebook, write about why that person is so successful, and how he or she has become such a success.

Lesson 40

Let's Talk...

Vocabulary

New Words

_____
_____
_____
_____
_____
_____
_____

Let's Talk Words

_____ _____
_____ _____
_____ _____
_____ _____
_____ _____
_____ _____

Usage

Look at all the vocabulary boxes from lessons 1 to 39. Write the words you don't understand in the boxes above. Walk around the classroom and compare your lists with other students'. Ask some students to help you learn the words in your boxes. Then help them with their words.

Let's Start

Form into small groups. Read the table of contents. Copy some topics into a category below. Then discuss which topics you enjoyed talking about and which ones you disliked. Explain why.

Liked	Disliked

Write about your experiences in this class. Whenever possible, use vocabulary words you have learned in this book. Share your story with a friend in class.

1. What other topics do you think should have been in the book? Why? What have you wanted to ask people in your class, but the questions weren't in the book? Ask them now.

2. Besides learning English, what else have you learned in your class that you believe will help you in the future? Explain.

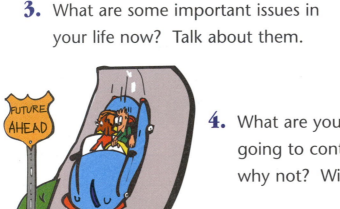

3. What are some important issues in your life now? Talk about them.

4. What are your plans for the future? Are you going to continue studying English? Why or why not? Will you look for a job? Explain.

Plan a party to say goodbye. Set a date. Decide the following: kinds of food, drinks, music, and entertainment. (Exchange ideas with your classmates from all of your countries.)

Verb Tense Chart

Infinitive	Past	Past participle	Infinitive	Past	Past participle
be	was/were	been	leave	left	left
beat	beat	beaten	lose	lost	lost
become	became	become	make	made	made
begin	began	begun	mean	meant	meant
bet	bet	bet	meet	met	met
blow	blew	blown	overhear	overheard	overheard
break	broke	broken	oversleep	overslept	overslept
bring	brought	brought	pay	paid	paid
buy	bought	bought	put	put	put
catch	caught	caught	quit	quit	quit
choose	chose	chosen	read	read	read
cost	cost	cost	rebuild	rebuilt	rebuilt
deal	dealt	dealt	ride	rode	ridden
do	did	done	ring	rang	rung
draw	drew	drawn	say	said	said
dream	dreamed	dreamt	see	saw	seen
drink	drank	drunk	sell	sold	sold
drive	drove	driven	send	sent	sent
eat	ate	eaten	sing	sang	sung
feel	felt	felt	sleep	slept	slept
fight	fought	fought	speak	spoke	spoken
find	found	found	spend	spent	spent
fit	fit	fit	spill	spilled/spilt	spilt
fly	flew	flown	split	split	split
forget	forgot	forgotten	spread	spread	spread
get	got	gotten	stand	stood	stood
give	gave	given	steal	stole	stolen
go	went	gone	sweep	swept	swept
grow	grew	grown	take	took	taken
hang	hung	hung	tell	told	told
have	had	had	teach	taught	taught
hear	heard	heard	think	thought	thought
hide	hid	hidden	understand	understood	understood
hold	held	held	wake	woke	woken
keep	kept	kept	win	won	won
know	know	known			

Index
The number after each word indicates the lesson number where the word first appears.

Answer Key

Lesson 2 Favorite Things
Usage page 5
1. dinner
2. favorite
3. child
4. play
5. go
6. sporting event
7. kind of
8. eat
9. breakfast
10. sport

Lesson 4 Transportation Systems
Usage page 13
(In any order) Answers may vary.

might	will
can	bus
encourage	train
native	government

Lesson 6 Job Interviews
Usage page 21
1. alphabetically
2. answer
3. ask
4. characteristic
5. company
6. employer
7. employment
8. file
9. fire
10. get
11. hire
12. interview
13. job skill
14. look for
15. prepare
16. question

Lesson 7 The Best of Everything
Usage page 25
1. shortest
2. variety
3. history
4. active
5. ago
6. sell
7. noisiest
8. saddest
9. nice
10. attractive
11. worst
12. explain

Lesson 10 Holidays
Think page 40

Thanksgiving   *November*
Eat a traditional turkey dinner with friends and family. Remember the Pilgrims (settlers from Europe to America) who thanked God and the Native American Indians for food in their new homeland.

Halloween   *October*
Children wear costumes and go trick or treating (ask neighbors for candy). Tradition stems from a Pagan ritual of hiding from dead spirits.

Independence Day   *July*
Have a picnic, and light fireworks. Celebrate independence from England.

Memorial Day   *May*
Bring flowers to the graves of American Soldiers who died during wartime. Honor the soldiers who died for the United States.

Dr. Martin Luther King, Jr. Day   *January*
To honor the memory of a great civil rights leader. His goal was to end racial discrimination.

Washington's Birthday   *February*
Close government offices. Remember the first president of the United States.

Veteran's Day   *November*
The President makes a speech. Government offices are closed. Sometimes there are parades. To honor the men who have served in the United States military.

Mother's Day   *May*
Take your mother out and buy her a gift to honor her.

Father's Day   *June*
Take your father out and buy him a gift to honor him.

Valentine's Day   *February*
Give someone you love (usually a spouse or boyfriend or girlfriend) a gift. To show your love.

New Year's Day   *January*
Parties the evening before and parades in the morning. Celebrate the new year.

Lesson 11 Superstitions
Let's Start page 41
1. bad luck
2. good luck
3. good luck
4. bad luck
5. bad luck
6. good luck
7. bad luck
8. bad luck
9. bad luck
10. good luck

Lesson 12 Sleep
Fill in page 48
1. lullaby
2. nightmare
3. good night
4. dream
5. sleep walk
6. go to bed

Lesson 13 Stealing
Fill in page 52
1. less
2. less
3. fewer
4. fewer
5. less
6. fewer
7. fewer
8. less
9. fewer
10. fewer
11. fewer
12. fewer
13. less
14. fewer
15. fewer

Lesson 14 Gossip
Usage page 53
1. news
2. false
3. spread
4. whisper, hear
5. wrong
6. fill, articles

Talk Your Head Off ■ 165

Answer Key

Lesson 14 Gossip
Fill in page 56
1. mouth
2. telephone
3. newspaper
4. magazine
5. radio
6. letter
7. note
8. television
9. friend
10. whisper
11. book
12. talk

Lesson 15 Ghosts and the Supernatural
Usage page 57
1. e
2. d
3. f
4. c
5. g
6. b
7. a

Lesson 17 Stress
Puzzle page 68

across
5. shout
6. read
8. walk

down
1. listen
2. shower
3. eat
4. exercise
7. talk

Lesson 18 Moving Children Out
Word Search page 72

```
d b w v s i b l i n g s r e g r e t a e m
o s i i s s u e x p l a i p e r b e e o
w c f t c h i l d r e n d u p r h s e v
n h e d e e t e f a m i v a a i l e e b o
o n y o u r o w n f a v i r r n i t e r u
f l r v e s l y s s h e c p e n u h c o t
a d r e g h u s b a n d e s n u h e h h i
m r r r e t k k b s s u e e t p l r i i
i a d u l t c h i l d r e n s a c r o s s
l n a t h r e a c t i o n y f a t h e r g
y k t y r l m o t h e r u s i s t e r j l
b d i m m e d i a t e f a m i l y e a d e
```

Lesson 19 Growing Old
Pronunciation page 76
1. t
2. d
3. t
4. t
5. t
6. d
7. id
8. d
9. id
10. t
11. id
12. d
13. t
14. d
15. id
16. t
17. t
18. d
19. t
20. t

Lesson 21 The Homeless and Welfare
Choose page 84
1. week
2. successful
3. steal
4. salary
5. jobless person

Lesson 26 Money Management
Let's Start page 101
1. $251.63
2. $3.71

Lesson 28 Government Spending
Usage page 109
1. ambulance
2. benefit
3. business loan
4. dental care
5. disability benefits
6. government spending
7. grants
8. highway
9. jail
10. legal aid
11. lighting
12. medical care
13. mentally ill
14. museum
15. primary
16. public
17. repair
18. require
19. research
20. sanitation
21. secondary
22. space exploration
23. street sign
24. unemployment benefits
25. wildlife

Lesson 31 Calling In Sick
Usage page 121
1. lunch break
2. call in sick
   sick day
3. average
4. day off

Lesson 34 What Would You Do If...
Usage page 133
1. f
2. c
3. e
4. b
5. h
6. g
7. d
8. a